A Gangsta's Demise

**Blueprint Publications
Presents
A Gangsta's Demise
A Novel by *Ja'Nai Ivory & Crusher***

Blueprint Publications LLC
P.O. Box 68804
Indianapolis, IN 46268

Copyright © 2015 by Blueprint Publications LLC

All rights reserved. No part of this book may be reproduced in any form or by electronic or mechanical means, including information storage and retrieval systems, without written permission from the publisher, except by a reviewer who may quote brief passages in review.
First Edition November 2015
Printed in the United States of America

This is a work of fiction. Names, characters, places, and incidents are either products of the author's imagination or are used fictitiously. Any similarity to actual events or locales or persons, living or dead, is entirely coincidental.

Blueprint Publications LLC
www.exclusiveblueprintpublications.com
Like our Blueprint Publishing page on Facebook:
www.facebook.com/blueprintpublishing
Cover design and layout by: Mario Patterson
Book interior design by: Mia Rucker
Edited by: Mia Rucker

Table of Contents

Acknowledgments

Introduction

Chapter 1

Chapter 2

Chapter 3

Chapter 4

Chapter 5

Chapter 6

Chapter 7

Chapter 8

Chapter 9

Chapter 10

Chapter 11

Chapter 12

Chapter 13

Chapter 14

Chapter 15

Chapter 16

Chapter 17

Chapter 18

Chapter 19

Chapter 20

Chapter 21

Chapter 22

Chapter 23

Chapter 24

Chapter 25

Chapter 26

Chapter 27

Chapter 28

Chapter 29

Chapter 30

Chapter 31

Chapter 32

Chapter 33

Chapter 34

Chapter 35

Chapter 36

Acknowledgments

Many accomplishments derive from ambition and restless determination. Along those same lines, there's a light inside of us that fuels each step. It's a common assumption that defines ambition as the urge to be successful. But for me, that's far from the mark. I could go on to mention a barrage of elements that'll make a case for reasons I should be seeking successful accomplishment. Yet, the aspiration behind my reason is completely different.

I want to dedicate this endeavor to my sons: Aaron, Cordarryl, Jonathan, Lil-Johnny, La'Jon, Enrico, and De'Angelo. Regardless of what you may interpret from those who know nothing of me, I need all of you to know that the word love could never define how I truly feel about you. It's beyond measure! I know I may have fallen short on showing unconditional love, and I understand how situations may have caused you to create some form of anger towards me. There's not a day that passes that I don't feel as though I failed you all completely. As years churn, it has become extremely difficult to instill the teachings of characteristic values through explanations and barriers. I know this is a small step, but I would like to show you that my efforts are forever inspired through all of you!

To Joseph, never should you wonder or stress about who will be there to catch you if you fall. Never drop your head through any moment of loneliness. I'm here for you. You will forever be my son!

And Mr. Larry Hoover, I'm smiling with you, Pops! I'll get rich or die trying! Your imprint is rooted to the core.

~Crusher~

I want to dedicate this to all of you who stood next to me in this fight through my growing pains without getting discouraged, finding my flaws overwhelming, or simply passing negative vibes. I quickly realized that this industry is very finicky and that all ideas are not suited for success. If I didn't have the support of family and friends, I'm sure the outcome would have been different. Yet I'm excited to tell all of you that my push to entertain is derived from your support. With that, I'll add that my love for you is amongst my highest regard for human nature. And along with my daily prayers for all of you, I thank you from the bottom of my heart. With love, I ask you to join me on the remainder of this journey. I promise it will be better than Disneyland!

XOXOXOXOXO

~Ja'Nai Ivory~

Introduction

Life tends to be an overcast of dilemmas that's uneven in its downpour. A funnel of flesh is bound by indifferences, making one decision the beginning of your last decision. It's the undying episode that is defined as reality.

Everyone has their own story created to be narrated, critiqued, and tailored so that the ending soulfully stops in misleading bliss. But not in the eyes of Ms. Siren Montago, her story is different. Some will deem her life story cruel, some will deem it harsh, others will claim unfair, and the rest will whole-heartedly say it is downright demonic!

Not Siren, her only demand is that you understand that all lives aren't favored for the romantic conclusion. Some are cruel, some are harsh, some are unfair, and even demonic! The saga that you are about to divulge and cast judgement upon is removed from the "happily ever after" inference. A bitch like Siren Montago will only explain this in one fashion, one form, and one time. Carry on…

Chapter 1

Piercing screams and howls echoed down the hallways of a Chicago psychiatric ward; cries of pain, cries of emotion, cries from crazed patients, more cries, and screams. To the sane, the setting could surely be described as psychotic. The heavily waxed floors and bright lights gave the hospital an eerie appearance.

"West wing corridor, one for discharge," a heavy-set black woman said into a walkie-talkie.

"Ten-four west wing," was the response.

The electronic locks unlatched with authority. The doors opened revealing another wing of the hospital most patients, if not all, could not remember going through because they were usually under psychotropic sedatives. The doors closed and the insane cries muffled down to nothing. This was the first time in five years Siren Montago had heard silence. She fidgeted nervously at the quietness. The only sound was the squeak from the shoes of the guard escorting her.

"Siren, are you ready for this?" the guard asked.

Siren returned the woman a very bland blank stare. The guard didn't even turn to face her.

"A lot of patients gather themselves and find that the world is a beautiful place…" the woman continued talking but Siren's thoughts were light years away from understanding what she was saying. For the past five years, all she'd had an opportunity to do was take medication and count the designed speckled flakes in the floor's tile. Their walk stopped at a door with a brass label on it. The name engraved in it read "Dr. Lucas Staple."

"Well, Miss Montago, this is the end of the road for me."

Siren just stared at the name of the door.

"I pray that you find your way in life, Miss Montago. I mean that dearly." The guard ushered Siren into the office and closed the door behind her. Siren looked back at the closed door.

"Miss Montago, please have a seat," Dr. Staple insisted politely.

Siren felt misplaced. She just stared at the doorknob.

"Siren?" Dr. Staple whispered.

She jolted at the whisper and backpedaled to the door. Fright filled her face. Dr. Staple removed his glasses, placing them on his desk.

"What's wrong, Siren?" he asked.

She clutched her hands together in a twirling rage. "I'm going home?" she asked with real concern.

"Yes, Siren. You've been cleared by the State of Illinois," Dr. Staple assured.

Siren began shaking her head in distaste. Memories of what home meant began to invade her mind.

"Is my father there?" she asked.

Dr. Staple looked confused. "Siren, your father has been gone since you were committed here.

"My mom, is she there, too?" she whined.

Dr. Staple smiled his sympathy. "Your mother passed away two and a half years ago. Remember the funeral?"

Silence crisscrossed between the two. A soft knock on the door broke through the silence.

"Come in," Dr. Staple sang.

The door opened and for the first time Dr. Staple saw a smile on Siren Montago's face.

"Eva," Siren excitedly sang, "Oh my God."

Dr. Staple was so happy for the recognition. He watched as the sisters embraced. Siren seemed extremely comfortable now.

"What are you doing here?" Siren asked her sister.

Eva's disturbed look spoke loudly.

"Where's mommy? Why didn't she come with you?" Siren asked.

Dr. Staple kept quiet. He wanted to see Eva's response, yet she looked at him for help.

"Siren, mommy did two years ago."

"What?" Siren sang. "How?"

Eva's eyes widened with concern. "Breast cancer, Siren, remember the funeral?" Eva asked.

"Ohhh," Siren sang. "I forgot all about it."

Eva was stuck.

Dr. Staple intercepted the situation. "Ms. Montago, I have some release papers that need your signature. In these documents, you'll see that Siren will be receiving a mental disorder payment of six hundred dollars per month. She'll also be required to remain on a low dosage of Chlorpromazine that'll ease her back to a normal state of mind," he explained.

Eva only half listened to the doctor's orders as he explained them. The monthly payment of six hundred dollars is what got her undivided attention. In her mind, the thought of seeing her crazy ass sister and dealing with the doctor was enough to make her snort a gram of cocaine right off of the doctor's desk. The meeting ended and the three of them walked out to the parking lot.

"Ms. Montago, if you have any questions, please, do not hesitate to call. My number is on the documents I gave you."

"Okay, Doc. We thank you dearly," Eva sang. She grabbed Siren's hand and they walked through the congested parking lot and out of the sight of the doctor.

Eva's smile faded and was replaced by a look of panic. Siren didn't notice. Her head swiveled in awe of the freedom she was experiencing.

They approached a car with a man leaning against it.

"Gotdamn, bitch! What the fuck took so gotdamn long?" the man barked. "I'm out here in this hot ass sun like I'm a trick or something. Bitch, get your ass in the car."

Eva looked at Siren, quietly praying that she kept quiet.

"This your crazy ass sister that you told me about?" he inquired.

"Siren, this is Lance. He's my boyfriend," Eva announced.

"Hell naw! Don't lie to the bitch. I'm yo pimp, hoe. Fuck you mean boyfriend?"

Eva dropped her chin to her chest. Siren couldn't digest the speed at which the events were taking place. She looked back and forth at the two in the front seat from her position in the back seat. Although the words were far from normal, there seemed to be no tension between her sister and her "pimp."

Siren looked through the window, taking in the enormity of the city of Chicago. After being away from the world for so long, each and everything they passed received her full attention.

"Siren? That's her name, ain't it?"

Siren looked from the passing city toward the driver's seat. Lance stared through the rearview mirror until their eyes met. Eva's piercing gaze was directed at the side of Lance's face.

"You know this is the free world out here?" Lance announced.

"Lance, please leave her alone," Eva begged.

"Eva!" he sternly countered as he skittishly looked from the road back to Eva as if on the verge of attacking her. She coiled against the passenger door.

"Bitch, you know better," he snapped.

Siren was shocked stiff, not knowing what to say or do.

"And in this free world, everything costs. Everything!" he continued. "Now your sister probably won't give you the full understanding of the life she's married to, so I'll lace you up in what's really good."

Siren's piercing green eyes bore through him as he spoke. In a scrambled array of memories, flashes of her childhood mixed with screams from the mental ward made her close her eyes tightly and shake her head in an attempt to rid her mind of the commotion.

"In this world, we are programmed to survive from the hard work put forth to eat. Some clock in at a job site and some own their own companies. There are drug dealers and free-loaders. Then there's me, one who provides satisfaction and entertainment to the hard workers. My job is to provide. Rather rain, sleet, or snow, my company has to be prepared to satisfy. That's the job of a pimp. I'm a pimp. And Eva is how we keep the hard workers satisfied."

"Eva," Siren whispered. "You're a prostitute?"

"Ever since mommy died, I was…"

Lance cut her off mid-sentence. "Don't start that Maury Povich shit, lying and shit," Lance snapped. "Let's keep it one hundred. You my hoe. Say it."

"I'm your hoe, daddy," Eva whispered.

At the mention of the word "daddy," Siren's eyes widened and her heart raced, accompanied by a nervous tick. She immediately had a flashback.

"Daddy, I don't wanna watch. Nooooo. I want mommieeeee!"

Her memory was extremely vivid.

"Shut up! Mommy isn't here and she doesn't know about this. If you tell, I'll kill your mommy! Now stop crying and touch it like daddy showed you."

"Pull over! Pull over! I'm about to throw up," Siren quickly cried out.

"Shit," Lance barked. "Man, don't throw up in my fucking car! I'm telling you."

Although threatening, he maneuvered toward the shoulder of the road as quickly as he could. He looked over his shoulder at Siren, who had hunched over in the backseat.

"Eva, make sure she don't throw up in the car, bitch," Lance barked.

Eva reached back to comfort her sister and instantly noticed a menacing scowl on Siren's face. They locked eyes for a telling second. Eva watched in slow motion as Siren sprang from the backseat with quickness and wrapped her shoestrings around Lance's neck, pinning him to the headrest. Siren pressed both of her knees into the back of the driver's seat for leverage.

"Siren," Eva yelled. "Stop it! You're killing him, Siren! Stooooppp!"

Eva tried helping, but the more she tugged at the shoestrings, the more pressure Siren applied. No one outside the car could see what was going on. Aside from the rocking of the car, it looked like just another normal day in Chicago.

"Eva, Eva, help me get him back here," Siren panted as she released the strings from around Lance's lifeless body.

Eva was completely stuck. She cried and flopped her hands back and forth in a frenzy. There were only two human beings whose murder she had witnessed. This was the second one at the hands of the one who had committed both of them. The first one was their father, and she had lied for Siren back then. That lie stood the test of time. A stream of tears flowed down Eva's face because life had just gotten tangled in a web of shit.

"Noooo, Siren, noooo," Eva cried.

Siren seemed to refuse to acknowledge her sister's rant. She continued to wrestle with Lance's body until she was able to get him into the backseat. The feat was strenuous. Her heavy breathing explained what she couldn't. Eva sat in the passenger's seat wide-eyed and paralyzed, but tranquil from the face of death and the calm of a killer.

"Eva, get in the driver's seat. Let's go. You don't have to worry anymore. Daddy can't hurt you like he did me."

Siren, that's not daddy," Eva screamed. "You killed daddy, remember? And I'm not about to let you get me in this one like you did with daddy. You killed him dead. You killed him, Siren," Eva screeched in frustration.

The crazed blank stare Siren gave Eva was unbelievable. There was no indication as to what was next. Eva panicked at the instant thought of Siren attacking her.

"Mommy said I was lying," Siren began. "Eva, are you saying that daddy didn't make me touch it?"

"Oh my God, Siren, do you understand what's going on right now? You just killed a gotdamn man! Look at him. You killed him!"

Instead of looking at Lance, Siren looked at the world outside the window.

"It's just me and you, Eva. Daddy's dead now. I want to go home." Siren looked back at her sister and their identical green eyes locked in a truthful stare.

"Let's go home," Siren whispered while reaching over and brushing her hand over Lance's wide-open eyes, closing them for good.

Chapter 2

"Oooohhh, Siren, that feels sooooo good! Your hands are so soft. Daddy loves you."

At fifteen years old, Siren knew something was definitely wrong with the sex acts her father demanded she administer on him. It had been five years of the same thing.

"Lift your shirt, Pineapple. I'm ready. I'm ready!"

She followed his orders.

"Push 'em together, baby," he whispered.

She bit back her grief, squeezed her developing breasts together, and grimaced at the steaming cum being splashed onto her.

"Oooohhh damn, Pineapple!"

Disgust kept her mute. She wanted to tell her mother but was afraid of what he may do to her. In the midst of her thoughts, a sharp knock at the bedroom door captured both of their attention. Her father looked down at her with a menacing scowl.

"You say anything and I'll kill you."

Siren jolted from under the bed sheets, eyes piercing through the dark room for her father. Her breathing was unsteady. It was a nightmare, yet she still frantically looked around in the darkness. A sigh of exhaustion funneled its way through her nose while beads of sweat rested between her breasts and on her forehead.

"He's dead, Siren," she whispered aloud.

After another exhale, she crashed back down onto her pillow. Thirst had found its cry. The nightmares always left her thirsty. It hadn't dawned on her that she wasn't in the ward anymore until a heavy banging echoed through the room.

"What the..." she whispered. "Eva? Eva?"

As she got up, she realized the tiled floors she was accustomed to were gone as her feet melted into the carpet.

"Eva?"

The banging aggressively persisted. Siren eased to the bedroom, unaware of how she'd even gotten in this house.

"Eva?"

The banging seemed to be getting louder and more annoying.

"Eva?" Siren whispered again.

She opened the bedroom door and the darkness of the rest of the house bore its brightness. Her eyes belted in all directions looking for an answer.

"Open this door, Eva. I know you're in there," a voice muffled through the front door followed by more banging.

"Eva, where you at? Eva!" Siren whispered frantically. Still there was no answer. Siren eased to the door and looked through the peephole. She snatched her head away from the glass eye at the sight of a man looking back at her. She withered in anxiety.

"Oh yeah, Joe?" the man screamed in warning. "This how you doin'?"

Siren held her breath. Had she been seen? She fought with the idea of taking another look. Silence churned from both sides of the door. The few seconds felt like forever. Her conscience prodded her to believe that the men outside the door had left. Instantly, she received a response that crumbled her thoughts.

"Ahhhh," Siren yelled as the door came crashing in from a hefty kick.

"Get that bitch," the man ordered the two other men who were with him.

Siren tried to run but her feet seemed to be clumsy and heavy. The intruders were too much for her. Her slender five-foot nine-inch frame was elevated with ease under the powerful clutch of one of the intruders. Every ounce of the one hundred thirty-eight pounds she retained was thrown to the matted carpeting.

"Turn over, bitch!" The demand was followed by a swift kick to her rib cage. Like a fish out of water, she flopped from her stomach to her back, more from the beastly explosion of pain from the kick than from her willingness to obey his order.

"Wait, wait," Siren pled. "What? What did I do? I mean, what do you want?" Siren's thoughts were bouncing around like ping pong balls. This was her first night away from the psych ward and the medicine was still funneling its retardant through her system as her eyes bounced from the faces of the men. *Is this a nightmare?* She wondered.

"Bitch," the leader growled through clenched teeth. With his foot pressed gently under Siren's chin, he began adding pressure slowly. "You will die right this fuckin' minute! Where's Eva?"

"Wait! Wait! I just got here today. I don't... I... I don't know anything. She's sleeping, I think. I don't know," Siren cried in panic.

"Funk, go check for that bitch!"

Siren looked up from the ground with a boot pressed against her neck. Her hands rested around the top of the boot. The intruder seemed larger than life.

"Joe, ain't nobody in here," Funk replied with light exhaustion from the search.

Siren and the intruder locked eyes. His downward gaze said nothing but translated into something so much more than words could express. His face slowly began contorting into a ball of madness.

"What happened to my brother? She kilt 'em, didn't she?" he growled.

"Your brother? I don't know what you're talking about."

"Lance," he snapped.

Siren tried swallowing from the ringing echo of the same name Eva had cried out. Flashes of Lance struggling under the grip the shoelaces had on his neck caused her to squeeze the intruder's ankle tighter.

"She kilt 'em and she's running. Sad part is she left you behind. What's your name?" he asked.

"Siren."

"Like the police?" he asked playfully.

"Yes."

"You kinda look like that bitch. You related to her?"

Siren's answers were on autopilot. "No! No, she's just helping me find somewhere to stay!"

A smile crept into the corner of his mouth. He looked at his two partners and then back at her.

"You just got evicted," he snapped.

His foot lifted from her neck and came powering down with purpose and aim.

The other two intruders joined in as if they were trying to ward off venomous snakes. Siren couldn't find her voice. The sound of bones cracking shocked her beyond reality. The rubber from the soles of the boots gripped her skin with aggression. Her sounds faded to mute. Pain no longer had a balance; it had gone its way. An orange flash blinked in sync with her heartbeat. Then all she could see was pure whiteness.

As her vision refocused, she sat upright and saw that her room was just as she had left it. A poster of T.I. was on the wall. Music played throughout the house. Laughter and squeals of glee filled the air. It was a common Saturday in the Montago house. Siren's excitement ruffled as she came to the realization that she'd awakened from a horrendous nightmare. Her bare feet padded down the hall as fast as she could move them. The music neared and a voice startled her. She rounded the corner into the family den and there her entire family carried on with life.

Siren watched herself. She reached up to touch her face and recoiled at the extreme coldness of her touch. Shock created panic.

"Mommy," she called out.

No answer. Siren looked on. Her mother was the prettiest person in the world to her. Her Indian ethnicity was evident. She had pretty, jet black hair with a glossy shine. Her face was soft with high cheekbones. She looked at her Dominican father. His face was rounded to perfection matching his signature five o'clock shadowed beard. His eyes were green and they gleamed whenever he smiled. Eva danced away while the small family cheered her on. Siren was ten years old again.

"What's wrong with Daddy's little princess? Siren, you look like you're not having fun," her father stated.

"I'm okay," she whined.

"You sure?" he countered.

Siren looked at her mother for a way out. She knew what was about to happen. Her mother was engulfed in entertaining Eva with her dance steps. Before Siren could think of anything to say, her father had picked her up and positioned her on his lap. She bit down on her lip in fear.

"Melody, why don't you go make us some pancakes? Anybody want pancakes?" he sang.

Eva led the way. "Pancakes! Pancakes! Pancakes!" she chanted. "Come on, mom," she added while tugging on her mother's arm.

"You and Eva will cook and me and Siren will clean the rooms," her father announced.

"No, mommy, no, don't let him take her, I mean me, back there. Please don't!"

Everyone broke off in different directions. Siren watched the younger image of herself walk down the hall hand in hand with the only man created to protect her. She shook her head helplessly as she followed with hopes of stopping the inevitable. She made it inside the bedroom before they could.

"Close the door, Pineapple," her father whispered.

Siren's younger self followed his instructions.

"Lock it," he stated seriously. His fun-filled expression had diminished. "Come show daddy what I taught you to do."

Siren watched as her younger image walked into his grasp.

"No! Noooo! No! This is wrong! Why can't you hear me, Siren? No, damn it!"

Siren turned in a rage to find something to throw and the mirror on the dresser revealed something she still couldn't comprehend. She looked at herself in the mirror as she watched her father insert his hand into the pants of her younger image.

"Noooo! Ahhhh! Stop it gotdamn it!"

Pain interrupted her vision. The home was gone and the pain intensified.

"Mommy," she fought to whisper.

Pain tore through her body at an all-time high. Siren's eyelids fluttered, followed by a wide-eyed shock of extreme pain. She was thrust back from the unconscious state she'd been beaten into.

"Wha... Wha... What?" she tried to say, but the brutality she'd undergone was paralyzing.

The home was engulfed in flames. Panic provided enough adrenaline for her to roll onto her side. She grimaced from the broken ribs she'd sustained and she could barely see through her battered eyelids.

"Ugh," she moaned from the pain.

Her jaw fell unhinged helplessly. Being so out of touch with her balance and equilibrium, she didn't notice the complete deterioration of her health until she reached her feet.

"Help me, Siren! Get me out of here! Get these ropes off of me! Hurry!" Eva yelled from a hogtied position.

At that second, Siren realized that her jaw had been shattered from the stomping of the intruders. She used her hand to raise the bottom section of her jaw as she moved toward Eva as fast as her body would allow.

"Hurry, Siren. Please hurry!" Eva cried.

Siren reached her, only to find that Eva had been hogtied with razor wire. Eva was lying in so much blood that Siren took a step back. In that moment, the window shattered from the extreme heat.

"Whoosh!" The air from outside hit the flames and they roared.

Siren shielded her face from the intense flames. The ceiling fan fell from the ceiling, crashing right behind her and igniting the hem of her pajama bottoms. The flames licked at her flesh like hungry hyenas.

"Ugh! Ugh! Ahhhh!" she screamed in agitation.

"Siren! Siren, please, pleeease!" Eva cried out.

Flames had rolled over to Eva's body. Siren shimmied out of her inflamed pajamas. She knew that she had to make an abrupt decision as she looked at her sister who had dug her out of the worst criminal and family judgement imaginable and saved her from life in prison for the cold-blooded murder of their father. Siren was undoubtedly indebted to Eva for life. Never would she have imagined that the return of the favor would prove to be as problematic as their current situation. It was in that moment that Siren understood that Karma and Life were sisters born from the same bitch.

Siren watched the flames grab ahold of Eva.

She screamed in a blood-curdling rant, "Sirennnn! Helllpppp!"

In only a wife-beater and a pair of panties, Siren ran in a full trot and dived out of the window head first. She lay motionless as the sound of the flames roared. Eva was screaming ferociously as the sirens of rescue units could be heard maneuvering toward the fire. The grass was cool and welcoming as an instant warning filtered through Siren's conscience. She realized that she was supposed to be burning to death with the only family she had left.

"Ugh," she groaned.

She got to her feet and stumbled off into the early morning darkness, unaware of the present and the future. But as she stumbled away, she knew that for the first time in her life, she would have to be the sole provider for Siren Montago. That reality was the realest shit any woman could possibly try to save herself from.

Chapter 3

"Devontay! Devontay! Come here! Look!"

The child ran as fast as he could in response to his brother's plea.

"What?" he huffed.

"Look!"

Devontay followed his brother's pointed finger with his eyes. "Wha... Oh shit!" he swore the instant he saw what his brother was stuck staring at.

Both of them stood stark still.

"Is that a leg?" Cameron, the younger of the two, asked.

"I don't know. It looks like it though," Devontay whispered curiously.

"Go see," Cameron countered in a whispering tone.

The challenge was a dare that the eldest brother could not duck. The title "big brother" gave off an aura of strength and toughness.

Devontay looked around the yard for something to prod with. His eyes locked in on a rake. He grabbed it and closed in on what appeared to be a human leg. Cameron followed close behind.

"Get off me, Cam," Devontay barked more from fear than anything else. He stepped up just close enough to the object to reach it with the rake and nudged it. Nothing happened. The brothers looked at each other.

"Let's pull it out of the bushes," Devontay suggested.

"Uhn-uhn," Cam whined.

"You a lil bitch," Devontay pouted.

"You a bitch, punk," Cam barked.

Devontay pushed his younger brother with all his might. Cam crashed to the ground but bounced back up with hate in his eyes. He charged at his older brother for revenge. Devontay stepped to the side and Cam's momentum forced him to trip over his own feet. His clumsiness landed him in the same shrubbery as the human leg. As he clawed at the air and anything welcoming his grasp, his brother's laughter stopped mid-chuckle.

"Cam! Cam, get out of there! Hurry! It's moving," Devontay yelled.

Once Cameron got himself out of the bushes, he stood next to his brother looking at the place where the leg had disappeared from. They could hear the rustling of whatever was in the bushes.

One hand appeared, and then the other. The boys took a slight step backward in unison. The two hands clawed a path through the shrubbery. The boys took another step backward as a head emerged from the thicket. When its face lifted from the ground, the shock, horror, and disbelief of the sight before the two children could only mute their cries. Both of their mouths hung in absolute dismay.

The creature didn't appear to be human to the boys. Blood that had dried up on its face made it looks sort of cartoonish. Its eyes were puffed in a purplish haze. Its cheekbones were nonexistent due to the swelling of its face.

But it was the way the bottom portion of its jaw hung lifelessly that sent the chill of horrid panic through the boys. The green slither of its piercing eyes topped off the crazed creature's crazed appearance.

"Daddyyyy! Daddy, it's a monster in the bushes! Daddyyyy," both of the boys yelled as they raced to the house.

Siren looked on as pain racked her body from the burns and fractured bones, not to mention the unbearable pain from her broken jaw. The shrubbery had been her shelter after the long journey she'd walked during the early morning hours. Her bare feet had taken the brute torture of the walk. The pain kept her thoughts on repeat. But one thing she knew to stay aware of was the fact that a run-in with the police would definitely send her back to the psych ward immediately. She'd committed murder, watched her sister burn to death, and been declared dead, all within twenty-four hours of being discharged from the ward.

The quick review of her situation got her to her feet. She had nowhere to go, but she knew if she continued running, wearing only a wife-beater and panties, she surely would end up in somebody's custody.

"Hey," a man yelled.

Siren looked back to see the two small boys and a man, whom she assumed was their father, trotting toward her. She tried accelerating but her fractured ribs refused to agree.

"Ugh," she cried, doubling over as the trio surrounded her.

"I told you, daddy. Look," Cameron boasted.

When the man saw the grave state Siren appeared to be in, he didn't know what to say or do. He stood over her with his hands raised in a harmless gesture.

"What happened to you? Why are you in the bushes? I mean, you need medical attention. Vontay, run in the house, get something to cover her up with, and bring me the telephone. Hurry up," his father demanded.

Siren had eased down to her knees from the agony. It pained her to breathe.

"Listen, my name is Demorris. These are my sons, Devontay and Cameron."

Siren looked up and closed her eyes. Flashes of her sister, Eva, being engulfed in flames filled her mind. Her eyebrows knitted in a furrow of pain as Demorris held his breath awaiting a reply.

"Here, daddy, I got it. I got it," Devontay sang as he handed his father the phone and a blanket.

"Do you need to call someone? Or do you need me to call an ambulance?" the man asked.

Siren shook her head, welcoming the blanket over her half-naked body.

"Listen, I'm not about to let you walk away like that. God forbid something happen to you after you leave here. Then I'd be involved. Uhn-uhn! What's your name?" He asked while turning on his phone.

The beep from the cordless phone made Siren perk her head up. She pushed her bottom jaw up with her hand. "No," she mumbled through her teeth. "Don't! Don't!"

Demorris paused in the middle of dialing 911.

"Please! I'm supposed to be dead."

"Huh?" Demorris asked. Had he heard her correctly?

"I escaped! I made it! They... They killed my sister," Siren pouted sadly.

"Who? Somebody tried to kill you? Cameron, Devontay, in the house! Now!" Demorris demanded.

"Awww, daddyyy," the boys sang in contempt.

"Go!" Demorris yelled. Then he watched his children run to security.

"What's your name?" he softly asked.

"Siren."

"And who is they? You said, *they* killed my sister," he inquired.

"I don't know. I don't know who they were. All I know is that they blamed my sister, Eva, for the death of her boyfriend, Lance," Siren explained.

Demorris recoiled in acknowledgement. He felt that it was not a good time to ask questions.

"So you don't want me to call help for you?" he asked.

Siren exhaled an unsteady shudder at the lengthy bout of misfortune she'd undergone.

"Uhn-uhn," she moaned.

"Well let me call my cousin. He knows a few black market doctors. Is that okay?"

Siren felt relieved and nodded in agreement.

"Come on. Let's get you inside and try to get you cleaned up."

Siren followed warily. She was given the opportunity to shower and get into some of Demorris' clothes. She got to see her reflection in the mirror and the sight of what had been done to her churned emotion. But the pain would not allow tears to form.

When she finished up in the bathroom, she stepped out and noticed a change in the demeanor of her savior, as well as the household. The sound of the boys playing was gone. The house was completely quiet.

Siren shuffled to the front room to find Demorris sitting on his couch staring at the blank screen of his television. She began to feel a bit of anxiety. She shuffled her feet clumsily for attention.

Demorris patted the cushion next to him, signaling for her to have a seat.

"Where's the kids?" she asked.

"Shhhh," he hissed. "Don't talk."

Siren's nerves erupted. She could sense something was wrong. "Humph," she countered.

"Shhhh," he replied.

Moments of awkward silence passed as Siren tried to figure out what was going on. Demorris, on the other hand, just waited. Suddenly there was a series of hard knocks on the door. Siren looked from the door to Demorris. He didn't even look at her, he simply answered the door.

When the door opened, Siren clutched the cushion on the couch.

"Aye folk, you lucky this bitch fell out in my backyard, nigga," Demorris snapped.

"Where she at?" the visitor asked.

Demorris opened the door wider and the visitor walked in. It was Lance's brother. He and Siren locked eyes.

"What in the fuck? How in the hell did she get out of there?" he asked aloud.

"Derrick, get rid of this bitch," Demorris snapped.

Derrick pulled a gun from his pocket and pointed at Siren.

"Nooo, nigga! Not in my gotdamn house, silly ass boy. Take that bitch somewhere," Demorris whined.

"Let's go, bitch," Derrick ordered, waving his gun toward the door.

Siren got up, not knowing how she would escape death from the same murderer a second time. Demorris refused to make eye contact with her as she walked by him. Siren tried to protest but he turned his head, ending her attempt.

"Derrick, man, make sure you get rid of this bitch. She knows where I live and the identity of my kids. Don't fuck up, man. Matter of fact, you need me to come with you?"

Derrick's face balled in anguish. "Miss me with all that. I got this shit," he pouted.

Demorris refused to respond to his younger cousin. He was relieved that the woman had found refuge in his backyard. Had she gotten to the police, the outcome would have probably landed Derrick behind jail bars. It was Derrick's arrogance that made Demorris shake his head.

"Get on this side," Derrick ordered, opening the driver's door.

Siren almost cried out from the undying pain that was racking her body while she climbed over the console that separated the driver and passenger seats. Derrick looked back at the spot where he'd left his cousin, Demorris, standing and they gave one another a head nod. Siren watched him flop down into the driver's seat and slam the door with venom. Then he gave her a deadly look.

"Can I say something?" Siren asked, pushing her jaw closed.

Derrick glanced over at her and then back at the road without answering. But Siren could see his jaw muscles tighten.

"For what, I don't know. But go ahead. Hell, even death row niggas get one last request."

"Why do I have to die for someone else's wrongdoings? I don't even know what's going on. All I know is that I'm getting the worst part of a situation that has absolutely nothing to do with me."

"Wrong place, right time is all I can say," Derrick answered.

Siren's eyes roamed like a student trying to decode a difficult lesson. She saw nothing that would assist her in an immediate escape.

"My brother is dead and I know that bitch Eva had something to do with it," he added.

"But you got her back! Why me?" Siren muffled through her teeth.

He gave her a sharp look. "No more questions," he snapped.

Siren focused on the reflectors glued to the median in the street. Her conscience began to whisper to her. There was no way she could have survived all she'd been through just to die. There was just no way. Just as her courage began to churn, Derrick's movement caught her attention. She looked over to see that he had removed his gun from his pocket and placed it on his lap.

"Fuck!" her conscience screamed. She did a triple take at the gun.

Think, Siren! Think, girl! She mentally coached herself.

She glanced around the floorboard for anything that could help her. She spotted something. The ashtray would be her answer and the contents inside the ashtray would be her weapon.

"Can I at least have something to smoke, my last smoke?" she asked.

Derrick seemed to be in a state of hate. He ignored her request.

Siren panicked. She glanced at the door handle, and then at the objects they passed. There was no way she would survive if she jumped out of the car.

"Here," he snapped, "and don't ask me for nothing else."

Siren would have smiled had her jaw not been destroyed. Derrick had tossed a Black & Mild cigar onto her lap. Siren had never smoked a day in her life. She placed the cigar between her lips, lifted her jaw to hold the cigar in her mouth, and lit it with her free hand.

Once it was lit, the ball was in her court. This was her only hope for survival. The gun lay awaiting anyone's grip. She took her hand from her jaw, ignoring the pain, and jammed the lit cigar in Derrick's eye.

"Ahhhh! Shit!" he screamed.

The car swerved on the highway at a speed of sixty miles per hour. Both of them tumbled left to right uncontrollably.

"Bitch," he yelled as he regained control of the car with his good eye.

The pain tore an array of thoughts through his mind. He pulled over to the shoulder of the road and slammed on his brakes, skidding to a halt. The event happened so quickly that by the time his hand reached for the gun, he realized that he'd reacted a second too late.

"Put your hands on the steering wheel," Siren declared through her teeth. The back of one hand pushed her jaw closed while the other held the gun on Derrick.

"I don't want to hurt you but I will. I need money. Give me the money in your pocket, now!" she demanded.

"Bitch, you burned my gotdamn eye," he cried out.

His ranting caused Siren to put a tighter grip on the trigger. She'd never fired a gun before but had seen enough movies to understand how it worked.

"Don't make me shoot," she whispered.

With a pained expression etched across his face, Derrick's hands managed to find the steering wheel.

"My fuckin' eye, man! This shit hurts!"

Siren ignored his pout.

"The money and I'll get out. No one has to get hurt any more than what has already been done," she promised.

Derrick removed a wad of bills from his pocket and tossed them onto Siren's lap. Now Siren had to choose between holding her shattered jaw and the gun, and opening the car door. Derrick waited in anticipation of her making the wrong choice.

Instantly, Siren pictured the identical scenario. With her back leaning against the passenger door, she opted for the door handle.

When she opened the door, the outside world came crashing in. Traffic was a mix of symphonic melodies with a twist of horns, squealing brakes, and music playing. She pushed the door open wider with her back. Feeling the freedom, she reached down and grabbed the money.

"Bitch!" Derrick grunted as he reached for the gun.

Panic fumbled clumsily through Siren's chest. Derrick had a grip on the gun. She was forced to let it go. Quickly she backpedaled out of the car, crashing hard onto the asphalt. She sprang to her feet ignoring the severe pain she was in. A gunshot echoed from inside the car.

"I'ma kill you, stupid bitch! I swear to Gawd," Derrick screamed, firing off another shot.

The second gunshot pushed a boost of get-up-and-go through Siren. The gasp of air she inhaled felt like a gallon of water being pushed down her throat. She was running off of pure adrenaline. She took one glance back and tripped over her own feet. Fright blocked her recollection of falling. All she knew was that she was that she was still running her fastest. Another gunshot sounded, causing her face to ball up in defeat.

"Stupid bitch," Derrick yelled, firing yet again.

The intersection was only feet away. Cars slammed on brakes watching the deadly encounter. Siren could only hear her heart beating. She could see her refuge just across the intersection. She dug her bare feet into the concrete and pushed for a faster pace. As the streets' intersection neared, she seemed to feel his breath on her neck. She darted into the intersection and before she could understand what was going on, a truck met her head-on. The truck slammed on brakes, followed by the rest of the cars. The driver hastily exited the truck.

"Oh my God! Nooo! Ma'am? Ma'am? Oh God! She came out of nowhere," he cried out to himself.

Siren lay unconscious in the middle of the intersection with the money she'd been holding scattered all around her. Blood oozed from her ears and her mouth lay agape.

"Oh God! Is she dead?" a bystander asked in panic.

Derrick didn't know exactly what had happened because he had given up on chasing Siren any farther after the last shot missed her. He heard the brakes screeching and figured life had just gotten unreal for him. He made it back to his car not knowing whether he should reveal what had happened or wait to find out if Siren would be able to identify them.

"Shit!" he screamed, patting gingerly at his eye. "Damn, Derrick, you let the bitch get away! Oh noooo!" he yelled at himself aloud.

Chapter 4

One hundred fifty-three days later…

The persistent sound of Siren's breathing machine hissed with each inhale and exhale. Joining in was the heart monitor with a constant beep. Medically, she'd survived, but only because of the technology of modern medicine. It had been almost six months since she'd been hit by the truck. A nurse checked in on her ever so often to make sure everything was fine.

As usual, nothing seemed disturbing. But then she noticed a stream of tears running down the side of Siren's face. The nurse jerked forward, poking her head closer to Siren's bed to get a better view.

"Oh God! She's responsive to memory," the nurse announced as she ran out to page a doctor.

Within minutes, she returned with a crew of nurses. By that moment, Siren's heart monitor was raging hysterically. The nurses ran in all directions to soothe the chaos. Upon settling the machines, one by one, each nurse froze in her tracks. Their Jane Doe lay with her eyes wide. The sharp green contrast of her eyes made the situation seem eerie.

"Nurse?" the doctor called out, hustling into the room.

"Dr. Roberts, look, she's out of her coma!"

"Ma'am?" the doctor called out to Siren. "Can you hear me?"

Siren looked over at the doctor. Everything seemed so bright and mysterious. The tube down her throat seemed to instantly become uncomfortable. Her memory shuffled like a deck of cards. At the thought of her sister dying in the house fire, her eyes widened in shock.

"Ma'am, I need for you to answer a few questions for me if you can," Dr. Roberts said while checking her vitals.

Siren just stared blankly.

"Do you remember how you got here?"

Siren shook her head in disagreement.

"Okay, that's fine," the doctor coddled. "By chance, do you remember your name?"

The thought of seeing the razor wire wrapped around Eva traumatized her thoughts. She shook her head no.

"Nurse, let's get this tube out of her throat. She seems self-reliant. Ma'am, you were involved in a very bad accident. You were fortunate to survive! You've been in a coma for close to six months now. The injuries you sustained have all healed while in your coma. Bring me her chart please, nurse."

Siren worked her mouth open and closed. Her jaw had been repaired. It was stiff but it worked.

"You throat will be sore for a few days," Dr. Roberts added, watching Siren massage her neck. "Can you repeat a few words and phrases for me?"

Siren agreed. Upon doing so, she found that her voice had changed. She tried clearing her throat but the sound was still there. It was a low husky whisper. She continued to repeat the doctor's requests.

"Can you sit up for me?" he asked.

The nurses in the room helped her sit upright. A slight dizziness had her off balance. She shook her head like a wet dog, and then cupped her hand over her eyes.

"I want to stand," Siren whispered.

The nurses looked at Dr. Roberts for confirmation. He nodded his approval. Her feet touched the ground and as she applied weight to her legs and feet, her joints cracked and popped.

"What's wrong with my voice?" she whispered. "Has it always been like this?"

"Your larynx was damaged and a partial tear in you vocal folds caused the low husky sound."

Siren tried to clear her throat again, but the strain remained tenacious. But trying to walk was an even harder task.

"Whoa! Take it easy, nurse," Dr. Roberts warned. "Remember she hasn't walked in almost six months."

"I'm fine," Siren assured. "It really isn't that bad. I just gotta…"

"Grab her, nurse! What's wrong with you?" the doctor's words seethed with anger. "You haven't listened to a single word I've said!"

Siren had collapsed to the floor in a heap. The nurses wrestled relentlessly to get her body back onto the bed.

"I'm okay! I'm okay!" Siren waved at the doctor as he checked her for injuries.

"I'm okay," she whined.

The determination in her voice expressed all her frustrations. Again, she rubbed her hand over her face. She pinched the bridge of her nose and when she reopened her eyes, her sight zeroed in on a "get well soon" balloon and a white stuffed bear. A card was positioned underneath the bears arm. Dr. Roberts followed her gaze.

"Oh! I almost forgot to tell you. The driver of the truck that hit you sent that. He left his phone number for you to call him if you'd like. He calls almost every week. He's genuinely concerned. There's also another gentleman that calls up here for you. He won't leave his name but he's intent on knowing if you've come out of your coma."

Siren's hand dropped to her lap. She was overcome with the thought of being chased with a gun and the eerie feeling of the electric shock that each shot fired at her back had caused.

"Also, the authorities would like to speak with you about the whole ordeal," the doctor added.

At the mention of the police, anxiety began trembling through Siren's body. She knew without a doubt that once she was identified by her legal name, the topic of Eva's death would surface and she would be remitted to the psychiatric ward for only God knows how long.

"You've got to get out of here, Siren," her inner voice reasoned.

"Can we wait before you call the authorities?" she asked. "I really don't have the energy to attempt to answer their questions, which I have no answer for."

"Unfortunately, they've already been notified. They should be here shortly," Dr. Roberts assured.

Siren looked at the hospital's identification band on her wrist. It read "Jane Doe." The meaning reminded her that she should be dead.

The nurses moved on autopilot.

"We need to run cat-scans and a few other tests on you to check for brain damage. You came out of your coma more vibrant than anyone else I've seen," Dr. Roberts announced with a smile.

Siren continued to stare at the name "Jane Doe." Moments later, she was being applauded by droves of medical staff as she was rolled down the hallway in a wheelchair. The moment was so great that her thoughts of death seemed to fade away. She just let her head hang with her chin on her chest.

Just less than three hours had passed and all the tests were over. She'd made a full recovery.

"Nurse?" Siren called out as she got out of the wheelchair. "Is there any way I can have a pair of shoes to walk in? I think that'll help."

"I'm not sure if I..."the nurse began to respond.

"Please, nurse," Siren cut in. "Please! My feet hurt walking with these socks on."

"I guess I can get a pair of orthopedic sandals sent here," the nurse answered.

"Thanks!" Siren replied with a smile.

Not many words were spoken thereafter between Siren and the medical help. Siren lay back in the bed that had been her home for the past six months. Her thoughts churned as she tried to figure out her escape route. She watched her nurse exit. But as soon as the comfort of isolation found her, the squawk of radio transmissions echoed from the doorway. She held her breath in an attempt to hear but her heartbeat was performing in dramatic fashion, making it hard.

"We received a call that the Jane Doe patient came out of her coma," an officer addressed the nurse.

The conversation was taking place just outside of the door. Although Siren knew she couldn't be identified, her heartbeat made her breathing unsteady as she lay frozen.

"Yes she did," the nurse excitedly answered.

"Do you think we could have a word with her?" the officer asked.

"Sure! She's this way."

The trio walked into the room. The two officers stopped at the door and watched the nurse. All three of them had confusion etched on their faces.

"I don't... I just left out of here," she stated aloud. "Where on earth could she have gone?"

The officers looked at each other and then back at the nurse.

"She can barely talk, let alone walk," the nurse panicked.

She stormed past the officers and out to the command center. The officers followed.

***

Siren struggled with each step, using the wall for support. She had hidden behind the bathroom door. She peeked out of the entrance to the room. The officers were huddled around the nurse's station. She lurched forward, scampering as fast as her weak legs would allow. The first place of refuge she saw was a laundry cart with bed sheets and patients' gowns. She pushed herself over the top, tumbling inside the cart. She burrowed under all the dirty laundry.

The chatter from the officers and the nurse had grown to another level. Siren could tell that others had arrived. Their concern was intense. After what seemed like an hour, the conversation concluded with the agreement to search the hospital for their Jane Doe.

Siren lay motionless. Questions began to trickle from places of reasoning. Did she even have enough strength to get out? She couldn't turn back. Her adrenaline began fading and she just knew the escape was worthless. She had no money, nowhere to go, and was wanted by two different groups who would inflict two different kinds of punishment, one was death and the other was jail.

As Siren started to climb from the bottom of the dirty laundry, the cart began to move. She froze like a cat. She could hear a faint sound of blaring music, which she figured must be coming from headphones. The sound of someone humming followed. There were periodical stops for laundry pickups before she heard the sound of the elevator's bell. The air eased out of Siren slowly as she relaxed into the dirty laundry. She had almost given up.

"Come on, come on! Slow ass elevator," the voice pushing the cart complained as he waited for the doors to close.

Siren could hear the rapid tap on the button he was pushing. The bell chimed again as she heard the sound of the doors sliding closed.

"Hold that door! Hold that elevator," a voice called out.

Siren stiffened like an ironing board. The blaring music from the headphones refused to allow the laundry attendant to hear the frantic request.

"Hey," the female voice yelled.

The doors jolted the whole cart as the nurse pulled the emergency bar, reversing the closing doors. Siren held her breath.

"Damn it, Jonathan! Turn those gotdamn headphones down, why don't cha!"

Jonathan snatched the Skull Candy ear buds from his ears. He could see the frantic look of concern on the nurse's face.

"Huh?" he countered.

"You have to turn that music down some. I was calling your name, yelling actually."

"Oh, I'm sorry, Bethany. What's up?" he asked.

"We're looking for a patient. She's wanted by the police for questioning. You remember the "Jane Doe" patient that was in the coma?" Bethany asked.

"Yeah, I heard she came out of her coma early this morning," he replied.

"She did. And I didn't think she could walk on her own, which makes it impossible for her to be alone. Someone may have come and taken her."

Jonathan's face balled in contempt. He appeared to be waiting for an explanation.

"No, seriously, Jonathan."

"Okay, so what do you want me to do? I mean…" he added with a shrug.

"Don't be so concerned," Bethany sarcastically stated. "Just make sure she isn't in that cart."

Sweat instantly formed in misty spots all over Siren's body. Silence filled the elevator for a long annoying moment.

"I'm not sticking my hand in this nasty ass laundry," Jonathan laughed. "If she's in there, God bless her soul. But seriously, I don't think she's in here," he added, kicking the mesh lining.

Siren tried her best to get as small as possible in the middle of the pile.

"Okay, but keep an eye out for her," Bethany warned.

The bell chimed again, the doors closed on the elevator, and Jonathan's music returned. Siren exhaled.

After the elevator ride and a couple twists and turns, the cart stopped. Siren tried listening for any sort of familiar sounds. Nothing registered. Moments eased by before her nerves had finally had enough. She clawed through the clothing and bed linen and looked out. She was in a hallway. The cart had been parked in front of the hospital's laundry room. Four other carts were parked around the one she was in. After a quick glance around, there was no one in sight. She fought her weakness to climb from the cart. She tumbled onto the tile in a heap. She felt so helpless and out of place but she had no time to waste.

Siren carefully collected herself and pulled up from the floor, using the wall. Her head swiveled from side to side as she walked. It started to register in her mind that her mission was impossible. Emotion began to ball up in her chest. Attempts to corral the tears were useless. The first tear fell heavily, followed by sniffles.

As Siren lifted her head in mock courage, she noticed that the hallway stopped at double doors. Once she reached the doors and looked out of the window on the door, she saw a glimmer of hope, an exit door. She held her breath briefly. The sight of an escape widened her eyes with sheer anticipation. Excitement motivated her feet to move forward.

"Please, let this be true, please!" she whispered.

Her fatigue was in full coercion of stopping her, but being captured was not an alluring alternative. She pushed the exit bar on the door and, to her relief, it opened. The night air was humid, a shocking contrast of the cool air inside the hospital. She felt daring as she ushered her tired legs along the wall outside. She had no idea where she was, but understood wholeheartedly that she'd gotten away yet again. A payphone was her only dilemma. She had to find one.

Once she made it to the street, she realized what the passersby were staring at. She was dressed in only a hospital gown. It seemed that she instantly became aware of her nakedness underneath the gown. Fear funneled through her veins with each step. To her delight, she spotted a payphone.

"Thank you! Thank you! Thank you!" she praised as she made her way toward the phone.

Siren looked down at the teddy bear she'd been clutching for dear life since she'd started her escape attempt. She retrieved the card that had been sent to her by the truck driver that caused her hospitalization. For a brief second, she just stared at the name and number. A car horn jerked her from the daze.

"Hey, Lady, are you okay?" a passerby screamed from his car.

Siren closed her eyes and waved her hand in dismissal. Quickly, she dialed the number collect. Then she listened to the operator's instructions.

"Hello?" the male voice answered after accepting the charges.

"Hi...Ummm... I don't know how to explain this but I'm the girl that was run over by you," Siren skittishly stated.

"Huh? Excuse me?" he responded.

Siren looked at the card, hoping for help.

"Ummm... I mean, I was told that you called the hospital about me every week, to make sure I came out of my coma."

"Jane Doe?" he asked excitedly. "I thought you were comatose! Oh my God! You're okay?"

"I know this may sound crazy but I'm being racked by some very bad people and I need some help," Siren explained.

"But I thought you were in the hospital?" he asked.

"I escaped."

Siren's reply stunned the man into complete silence.

"Hello?" she whispered after a few seconds.

"Oh, yeah, yeah, I'm still here. I... I... I just... I just don't... I'm trying to understand what's going on," he countered with wonder and uneasiness in his tone.

"I'm so sorry! It's a very long story. But I don't have time to explain right now. I really don't know how long I'll live out here in these streets. You're the only hope I have," she explained.

"What can I do? What do you need me to do?" he asked nervously.

"Can you pick me up? I have no money, no family, and no clothes!"

"No clothes?" he asked totally confused.

"I had to escape from the hospital. I only have on the gown they give patients."

"Okay! Okay! Where are you?" he asked.

Siren read off the address of the building in front of the payphone.

"Don't move," he barked. "I'm on my way!"

Siren placed the phone back into its cradle. What she didn't know was that she'd just made the phone call of a lifetime. Never could one imagine a snowball effect as dominant as the one she was now in the middle of. As she locked her eyes on the name on the card, the only thought running through her mind was whether the man was going to be a blessing or a curse.

Siren found refuge behind the bay of payphones for the next half hour. She was beginning to get impatient when she spotted an all-black Lexus GS-350 slowing to a complete stop in front of the bay of payphones. The sleek style of the automobile sent waves of comfort through her as she assumed her savior had arrived. She stood so she could be seen but before she could take a step toward the car, it lurched back into traffic without a stutter.

"Oh nooo! Hey!" Siren yelled as loud as her soft voice would allow.

She walked toward the fading headlights. In that instant, she saw high-beams flickering. Her chest constricting, knowing it was the police. Her head hunkered as low as it could as she walked back toward the payphone. She refused to look up.

"Jane Doe? Jane Doe? Is that you? It's me, Carlos."

Siren's head peeked toward the voice. She saw him and panicked even more because it dawned on her that she had no clue what he was supposed to look like. She'd envisioned an image, but it was not the same image that was looking back at her.

"Jane Doe? It's me," he pled. "Get in! Hurry!"

Second guessing was no longer an option for her. She withdrew her uncertainty and got into the truck. At the first sight of her green eyes, the driver's mind wandered aimlessly in a moment of enchantment.

"My God, you're beautiful," he whispered aloud.

Siren broke the stare while blushing as the truck pulled into traffic. They knew nothing about each other, which made the closeness very uncomfortable. Siren decided to be the first to explain.

"I'm sorry to involve you in this situation," she began, "but you were the only chance I had of surviving."

"Surviving?" he questioned. "It's that bad, huh?"

Siren glanced at him quickly and then back out of the passenger's window. She told him everything, from the discharge from the psych ward to being chased into the grill of his truck. She'd left out the people she'd killed and let die. Carlos felt extremely bad for her mishaps. Her beauty played a major role in his sympathy for her.

"So what is it that you need me to do?" he asked. "I mean, what can I do? It seems that you're wanted by some bad people and I'm not willing to just drop you off somewhere, knowing that you may be killed. Hell, keeping you away from trouble is the least I can do after almost killing you myself. Damn, there's no family you can lean on for help?"

Embarrassed, Siren closed her eyes and shook her head in disgust of her situation.

"I'm all that's left. They're all dead," she answered.

Her answer had an eerie aura about it; Carlos felt it in every syllable. Not knowing he was in the company of a stone-cold murderer, he opened up his resources.

"I have only one option for you," he began. "I have a cousin down in Orlando, Florida. She's not your typical girl, though. She's a party animal!" he assured. "But if you that going down there will help, then I'll send you down there. Hopefully you can get yourself together and start over. What do you think?" he asked.

"Florida?" she replied.

She'd never left Chicago, let alone the state of Illinois. She knew absolutely nothing about Florida but the really had no choice.

"When?" she asked.

"The sooner, the better, right?" he countered.

She looked over at him once again. He had his phone in his hand, dialing a number. He returned her stare in between driving and dialing.

"Alexia? Hey, this is Carlos."

Siren could tell Alexia was excited to hear from her cousin by the way Carlos smiled.

"I need a very, very important favor. It's really dear to me."

Siren returned her gaze to the sights out the window.

"I have a friend who needs to stay with you for a while. I'll pay you monthly for her cost of living. Don't worry, but it's an emergency," he pled.

A pause in the conversation got Siren's attention. She looked over at Carlos. He had a deep crease of concern across his forehead.

"Tonight. I'm putting her on the Greyhound tonight. Please, Lexi, for me."

A smiled lifted his cheeks. He abruptly put the phone on his thigh to cover the receiver. "What's your name?" he asked hurriedly.

The truth seemed to be stuck in her head. She had lied so much but she figured this was the time to let the truth fly.

"Siren," she whispered. "Siren Montago."

She watched him repeat her name. Something in the pit of her stomach screamed that she'd just made a mistake that would haunt her drastically.

Chapter 5

"Welcome to Gentlemen of Distinguished Nature Publications! How can I assist you?"

"Yes, I'm Alexia Campbell. Ummm... I was scheduled for the viewing of my photo layout, along with my interview for the spring edition."

"Okay, Ms. Campbell, who was your photographer?" the security guard asked.

"Cedric Jones," Alexia replied.

"Location?"

"City Walk, down in Universal Studios."

The receptionist's fingers rummaged the keyboard. Alexia was in complete awe of the confines of the Gentlemen of Distinguished Nature office. It was located in a plaza off of Colonial Drive, which was in a decent area. The decorations were of immaculate taste. The all-glass interior seemed to just yell "class."

Alexia rubbed her fingertips along the ribbon-stripped, mahogany veneer desktop. The sublime wood furniture matched the large marble tile. The office was pure luxury.

"Here we are, Ms. Campbell," the secretary announced. Why don't you have a seat while I get our interviewer for you?"

Within minutes the secretary signaling for Alexia to follow her. She was led to a conference room. Once she crossed the threshold of the door, her breath got short.

"Oh my God," she beamed.

Looking around the conference room, she was at a loss for words. Her photo spread was projected onto a wall. The room was dimly lit, which illuminated the pictures.

"Ms. Campbell, I'm Trey. It's a pleasure to meet you. Welcome to GODN Publications. Have a seat, beautiful."

Alexia seemed to float in his direction. She'd been warned about being pampered by photographers in exchange for sex, but she quickly understood how a bitch's legs could mysteriously find themselves invitingly wide open. She swiftly assessed Trey from head to toe. He had a business-like swag. From a glance, he seemed to be strictly about business as he sat on the edge of the desk.

"GODN is an acronym for Gentlemen of Distinguished Nature. Here at GODN, we find class to be the lead of what we stand for. It's not about the prettiest face, the fattest ass, nor the quickest fuck. We're bigger than the typical publishing company. GODN is the founder of recording artists, clothing lines, novels, and most importantly, loyalty. Are you following me thus far?" he inquired.

The groupie in Alexia nodded in agreement like an eager child.

"Keep in mind, Ms. Campbell, that we are interested in exploiting your flaws. Here, we strive to fully expose you. What I mean is, the more we can get out of you verbally in this interview to match your beautiful pictures, the more likely it is for you to become a household name. Honestly, you want the readers of your interview to get aroused by the visual you paint through words while they're looking at your pictures. This allows them to instantly mentally create situations between you and them, sort of like an intimate one night stand. Does that make sense to you?"

"Oh yes, I understand fully! I'm ready!" Alexia countered with excitement.

In that instant, her phone chimed. They both looked at her bag. She quickly reached for her phone.

"One second," she said. "Hello?"

A few seconds lingered before she responded. "Are you serious? Like right now? She just got here?" she pouted.

Trey could sense the untimely grief as Alexia looked up at him.

"Busy isn't even the word! Busy is an understatement," Alexia continued.

Trey acknowledged her problem with a head nod.

"Hold on," Alexia said into the phone. "Trey, I'm sooo sorry! My cousin sent a friend of his down here to live with me and she just arrived at the bus station."

"Just tell her to catch a cab to 2221 West Colonial Drive and she can wait in the lobby while we finish."

Alexia relayed the message and then ended the call.

"Now let's get started," Trey said. "I'm going to ask you a series of questions and your answers will be printed. So choose your words carefully."

A light tap echoed off of the conference room door.

"Come in," Trey invited.

The door opened and in walked the owner and CEO of the GODN brand. He was dressed in an all-black Ralph

Lauren suit. Alexia immediately noticed the change in Trey's demeanor. Alexia's smile beamed between the two men. The owner didn't say a word. He simply took a seat in the corner of the conference room.

"Who's that?" Alexia asked.

"The owner of all this," Trey answered. "Now let's begin."

Trey began recording the interview.

"Is Lexi your real name? Or is it your entertainment handle?"

"Lexi is short for my real name, Alexia."

"Okay, Lexi *'Tha Body,'* please tell us what city and state you're representing."

"I'm from Atlanta, Georgia. But I was raised right here in the FLA."

"Is this your first magazine layout?"

"Yes, my first, but far from my last. I'm here to stay…"

"Trey!" the owner called out. "Stop recording! Stop!"

Lexi and Trey both swiveled in his direction.

"That's not GODN swag! We're not trying to be just another magazine. When people read these interviews, we don't want to bore them with just words on a page. Look at the layout. Her pictures don't require and abundance of explanation. What needs to be unveiled is what her pictures don't foretell. A pretty face and fat ass is worthless over here.

What we're branding is obsession. We want people to find an obsession about Ms. Campbell, an obsession that will follow the reader to bed and to their job site the next day. We need something that'll either motivate the reader to do as Ms. Campbell would do, or make them share Ms. Campbell's story with others. Always remember, intellect solidifies common sense."

Both Alexia and Trey were stuck on his approach, stuck because it made complete sense.

"Now look, we all know that sex sells. The imagination gives us an automatic visual. Look at Ms. Campbell's pictures. A nigga laying in his bunk in a federal prison somewhere looking at these pictures don't need a caption because the picture alone causes him to think of every way he could fuck her to sleep. It's worthless to say 'she likes it from the back' when in fact she has a back-shot with the camera only inches away from her ass. Again, intellect solidifies common sense. Ms. Campbell, you probably the extent of who I am, actually. But if I asked you to describe this building, this company, using only one word, what would you say?" the owner asked.

Alexia looked him up and down in admiration.

"Luxurious," she answered.

"Trey, make this interview luxurious!" he announced. "I'll step out now. Ms. Campbell, it was nice meeting you. Welcome to GODN."

Alexia watched the unknown figure walk to the conference room door. She couldn't dare allow him to walk away without at least knowing his name.

"Excuse me," she called out. "What do I call you?"

"BOS. But the streets call me Crusher."

His response sent an eerie chill through the room. His last comment said much more than Alexia could likely fathom.

Chapter 6

Siren placed the payphone back into its cradle. Standing inside the Greyhound bus terminal, she could only watch as the bustle of patrons walked about purposefully. The Sunshine State, a place she had never considered visiting, was now under the soles of her shoes. She smiled at the thought of being out of Chicago. The feeling was a relief. She collected the belongings that Carlos had bought for her and made it outside of the terminal.

The sun beamed like a melody of colors that seemed to welcome Siren to a long-term vacation. Not realizing that there was an ocean nearby, she felt what seemed to be a tropical breeze. The grass was a beautiful shade of green. The trees were vibrant. There seemed to be no tension in the air. In fact, Siren had to push her feet to begin walking into a new life. The address that Alexia had given her rested in the palm of her hand. She glared at it, not knowing what would come of the relationship between her and a woman she knew nothing about.

As Siren hailed an awaiting cab, there was one thing in particular that she knew she had to wholeheartedly accept and that was the fact that she had to survive by any means necessary. As grim as life had been for her since she was a young girl, she refused to bow out willingly.

The cab ride was short.

"This is your destination, miss," the Haitian cab driver announced.

Siren paid, gathered her belongings, and got out of the cab without another word.

"Welcome to Florida, lady," the cab driver added as he pulled away.

Siren watched as the cab sped off onto the Floridian highway. The building she stood in front of was very sleek.

"GODN?" she questioned aloud.

She glanced at the address that she had written on her hand.

"2221 West Colonial Drive," she read while matching the numbers on the building to the numbers on her hand. "This is it," she said.

After another glimpse at the address, she walked inside the tinted double doors. The first thing that caught her eye was the wall full of assorted plaques ranging from gold and platinum records to Grammy awards. Her head twisted in amazement.

"Welcome to Gentlemen of Distinguished Nature," the receptionist greeted with high spirits. "How can I help you?"

Siren fumbled over her thoughts briefly all while trying to find the proper words to say.

"Ummm… My friend told me to catch a cab from the bus station here and wait. She said that she was in some kind of interview," Siren explained.

"Ma'am, you can speak louder. It's okay," the receptionist assured.

Siren smirked graciously and walked closer. "I can't. This is the loudest I can speak," she said before repeating her reason for being there. "Her name is Alexia Campbell," she added.

"Oh yes, she's in an interview right now. Uh, I guess you could wait in our lobby for her. She should be out within an hour or so."

The sound of hard-bottom shoes crashing against the marble tile cut through the office. The sound grabbed the attention of the receptionist, while Siren turned her attention to the spectacular design of the office; the approaching footsteps drew no concern from her.

"Shannon, I'm about to step out for lunch. I need you to pull up the sales for the last six months and draw up a cover page indicating the contents of the report. Try to have that done by the time I return."

"No problem, sir. I'm on it right now," Shannon agreed.

The male voice grabbed Siren's attention. She turned around and caught sight of the person behind the orders. He hadn't even noticed her standing in the lobby, or so it seemed, that was until he looked up from the receptionist. His glance over at her resulted in a triple take. Siren turned her head to avoid any attention. Her head swiftly scanned past the receptionist's desk as though something had grabbed her attention. But he was still staring at her.

"Excuse me," he called out. "Is there something I can help you with?"

"Oh, she's waiting for…" the receptionist began but was cut short when her boss raised his hand toward her.

Siren pretended she didn't hear him. She was in a very bland mood. The long bus ride from Chicago was a bit extreme for her.

"Excuse me, miss," he called out again.

"Oh, are you talking to me?" Siren asked, dumbfounded.

"Very much so," he replied. "You're the only one out here."

Siren rolled her eyes in contempt for his cockiness. "I'm waiting for my friend. She's in some kind of interview."

They both stood at a distance, in more ways than one.

"That's fine. I was just assuring that you had been taken care of and wasn't just out here unattended."

"I'm okay," she answered.

They paused and the moment lingered.

"I'm the owner of GODN," he added while extending his hand.

Siren looked at it as if it were a trick. She looked from his hand to his eyes. In that instant, she couldn't quell the voice inside her head the second their eyes met. There was a story in his eyes. The unmoving, pitch black pupils stared at her. Reluctantly, she met his hand with her own. She recoiled slightly. The inside of his hand was cool and callused. If she would have had to compare its texture to something, it would definitely have been the likes of grabbing a cinderblock.

"Are those contact lens?" he asked.

She shook her head in disagreement. In the midst of admiration, Siren was relieved to see another woman approaching them.

"You must be Siren," Alexia announced.

Her strut toward them was purpose driven. To Siren, it looked as if Alexia was practicing some type of hip exercise by the way she swayed her hips.

"And you must be Alexia."

"I see you found Mr. Crusher," Alexia flirted.

A slight scowl creased the corner of Alexia's mouth as she noticed the way he held on to Siren's hand.

"Yeah, he was just introducing…" Siren began.

"So, Mr. Crusher," Alexia sassed, cutting Siren short, "what can I expect after this process?"

Alexia glanced quickly back at Siren and purposely swung her hair in haste.

"Professionalism, Miss Campbell," Crusher added. "Here at GODN we don't exhibit anything less. Professionalism is the key, and success is the mission. Anything less is dismissed. This is a milestone, and you're in the making of something historical."

"I'm definitely ready for the next phase," Alexia eagerly replied.

"It was my pleasure meeting you two today. Miss Campbell, I wish you much success with your career and future endeavors. And again, you are?" he asked Siren.

"She's my cousin's friend. He asked if she could come stay with me because she's homeless. Plus, my cousin knows I'm super responsible," Alexia answered quickly.

Siren's face turned burgundy with embarrassment.

"Your name is?" he asked again with persistence.

"Siren," she answered, glancing down at the tile.

"It was nice meeting you both," he said while backpedaling his departure.

"You probably don't have much with you," Alexia continued badgering while still in earshot of the owner of the company, a man who she deemed a prospect to help her get to the top. "You ready?"

Siren had no leverage to use in an argument at the moment so she forced a counterfeit smile and followed the woman who would cause her more havoc than she'd undergone in Chicago.

"Have a wonderful day, ladies," the receptionist yelled as the two ladies walked outside.

"Girl, where you get them cheap ass shoes from? Walmart?" Alexia asked Siren.

"I don't have nothing, Alexia," Siren shrugged.

"Pretty as you are, girl, you haven't learned about the mechanics of that juice box between them long legs?" Alexia nagged.

A car horn broke through the stronghold Alexia had on Siren's attention. They both looked in the direction of the horn to see an all-black, two-door, convertible Bugatti Veyron

Grand Sport trimmed in gun-metal grey. The car alone made breathing difficult for Alexia. But for Siren it was a totally different feeling of yearning. A yearning that she couldn't quite define at the moment, but she knew that sex wasn't going to fulfill it.

Crusher nodded as he crawled into the traffic. Alexia and Siren followed his exit with their eyes.

"First off," Alexia began, "welcome to Florida, girl, home of the sunshine and the land of plenty, plenty, plenty money! I don't know what's going on in Chicago. But down here, ballers ball and women search for that one meal ticket. Men down here pay for what they want. There's no pimps and crazy shit like that. It's simple down here. The motto is *get in where you fit in*."

Siren listened but was mostly focused on the bright settings alongside the Floridian highways. It seemed as though every color told its own story. The brightness made her want to be upbeat and happy. She looked over at Alexia, who was babbling away. Had Alexia known that a stone-cold murderer was occupying the passenger seat, Siren was almost sure that the conversation would have been of a totally different nature. From what Siren could decipher from the conversation, the priority was money and the mission was to get it. She glanced at Alexia and forced a phony smile, nodding every so often.

"With all that being said, what you know how to do?" Alexia asked.

"What do you mean? I'm lost," Siren truthfully replied.

"Biiitttccchhh," Alexia sang. "You haven't heard one word I said! Bitch, what's your hustle? What do you do?

Dance? Fuck? Steal? What? I know you don't work because your ass came down here broke and busted. You got to know how to do something to get paid."

Siren silently repeated the list of things Alexia considered a hustle. "Dance? Fuck? Or steal?" her mind repeated. "Dance? Fuck? Or steal?"

She found no comfort in any of those hustles. The more Alexia talked, the more Siren knew she'd made a terrible decision by coming to live with her.

"Actually, Alexia, I don't have those types of capabilities to do any of those things."

"Capabilities? Bitch, everybody capable of laying on their back for a few minutes to cash out! Broke bitches call it tricking but a hungry bitch calls it eating. These tender dick niggas damn near bust their nut before they can get the dick in good. A little fake moan and call 'em daddy, you got 'em eating out of your hand," Alexia assured.

At the mention of "daddy," Siren's nose flared and her heartbeat picked up. Anxiety caused her breathing to falter from its original pace. Alexia didn't notice. Flashes of her dad touching her sent chills down her spine. Alexia continued babbling about sex and how easy it is to trick. Siren grabbed ahold of the door handle to stabilize herself.

"No!" she snapped as loud as her voice would allow.

Alexia stopped talking in the state of shock. She looked from the road to the passenger seat.

"No? No what?" Alexia asked.

"Fucking? Prostituting my body? Calling him daddy? No!" Siren barked.

"Okay. Well, bitch, you gotta do something to pay your way. Hell, I don't know what my cousin told you about me, but my income is made by hustling, and there are no limitations on what I'll do to get paid. Now if you ain't with the program, then... then... I really don't know what to tell you."

They both fell silent. Neither of them could fully process what the other was saying.

Alexia's mind was telling her, "This bitch needs to get with the program."

Meanwhile, Sirens mind screamed, "Another dumb ass suggestion about being a gotdamn prostitute and I'll kill her dead."

"My only other suggestion is that I can pay for you to go back to Chicago and deal with whatever it is you're running from. I don't know. Let me know something," Alexia said, breaking the silence.

"No, I can't go back!" Siren blurted mistakenly.

Again Alexia looked over at Siren. She instantly began to wonder what Siren was really running from.

"Why?" Alexia asked.

"It's nothing. I... really... It's nothing," Siren stuttered.

Alexia slowed the car and veered to the shoulder of the road.

"You're lying," Alexia snapped.

"Is it that obvious?" Siren asked.

"Girl, you gotta tell me what you got me and my cousin in the middle of because, for my cousin to ask me for a favor like this, I know you were in a serious bind. Now you really do need to tell me who and what I'm hiding you from."

Siren took a deep breath. She knew the truth would require her to start from the murder of her dad, and providing all of the information from her father's death up until the present would undoubtedly get her turned over to the authorities.

"Okay. The truth is I was dating this drug dealer and he thought that I stole his money," Siren began.

It was a complete lie, a lie that would come back to cause enough havoc for blood to be shed. But at the moment, it seemed absolutely harmless.

Chapter 7

Trouble in the city…

"What the fuck do you mean? Make me understand exactly what it is that you're saying because I'm finding it hard to digest the bullshit you keep trying to feed me!"

"I don't know. All I know is that they said she's no longer in the hospital. She must've gotten some help or something because they did say she came out of her coma," he added while rubbing the burn scar around his eye.

Derrick knew the predicament he'd been put in since Lance had been found strangled to death. But things had gotten much more intense for him because he'd allowed the only witness to their retaliation to escape on three separate occasions.

"Listen, Derrick, the board is breathing down my neck, questioning the leadership of my hood."

"But Mitch, I'm doing all I can to get this bitch," Derrick complained.

"You ain't doing it right then, fam," Mitch snapped.

"What you wanted me to do, run up in the hospital on some kamikaze shit?" Derrick's agitation spewed.

"You gotdamn right, nigga. Fuck! You asking me questions when you should be questioning your thought process. How you let a bitch run past you like she Desean Jackson and shit? For real, for real, fam, you got a nigga questioning your capabilities," Mitch calmly added.

"After all the work I put in, now you talking about my capabilities? For real, Mitch?"

Silence took up residence in their hostility.

"Decisions are on the table, Derrick."

"Decisions? For who?" Derrick asked timorously.

"The clock has started on you, Dee. You gotta find that bitch, bro, or they have to do what their literature has set before them on situations like this," Mitch humbly explained.

"Just like that, huh?" Derrick countered.

"Find her, bro! Go out and get that bitch!" Mitch ordered.

Derrick eased the phone from his ear and dropped it onto his lap. Concern flooded his every thought. He couldn't understand how all of this turmoil had landed on his shoulders. He'd done everything he could to capture the girl. He shook his head in disbelief. The tables had turned and the "X" was positioned right on the front of his forehead.

"What did he say?" Derrick's right hand man, Funk, asked.

Derrick didn't even take his eyes off the wall when he responded. "I gotta find that bitch or the board ordered me dead," he whispered.

"What?" Funk barked, jumping to his feet. "What kind of shit is that? Mitch said that?"

Funk's barrage of questions mounted to one conclusion, a conclusion that Derrick didn't have to explain any further. They both silently surfed their mental channels for a solution.

"That's some crazy ass shit right there," Funk barked in haste. "This can't be our life, man! So what if we can't find this lil bitch?"

Derrick cut his eyes at Funk. In return, Funk shook his head disapprovingly. Derrick gnawed nervously at his bottom lip, trying to think. But all he could come up with was a vivid vision of the girl's bright green eyes. He knew that if he ever saw those eyes again, he would actually be able to continue to enjoy his life. His only setback was that he had no idea how in the hell to start searching for someone he knew nothing about. Then all of a sudden, he jumped to his feet.

"Come on, Funk. Let's go. Let's go!" Derrick excitedly yelped.

"What's good, fam?" Funk asked in a state of wonderment.

"I got an idea! We might can find this bitch faster than we think!"

"How?" Funk countered.

"The cemetery…"

Chapter 8

The unknown tumbles…

"Wait a minute! This can't be the address."

He looked from the file in his hand to the charred remains of a house. Crime scene tape waved loosely, obviously because it had been up for too long. He put the car in park and leaned back against the seat. He tried to gather his thoughts and figure out what could have happened. With nothing forming by way of an explanation of the house's current condition, He got out of the car and approached the burned home. He just stood there trying to figure it all out.

Since Siren Montago had been discharged from the ward, he was confident that she would transform into a responsible citizen. But when she failed to call for her six-month assessment, he began to worry about her. He tried calling the phone number left in her file and he soon found that the number had been disconnected. Recalling how harsh the streets of Chicago can be, he began to shake his head.

"It's a shame what happened to that girl," a woman's voice blurted.

He jumped, startled by her presence. "You scared the daylights out of me," he huffed.

"Oh, I'm sorry. My name is Phyllis," she added, extending her hand. "I live across the street."

"Lucas Staple," he countered. "Nice to meet you."

They both turned their attention back toward the charred home.

"What happened here?" he asked.

Phyllis looked at the file in his hand. "You some type of house specialist or case worker?" she asked.

"No. No, I'm a psychiatrist."

"Crazy doctor?" she countered.

Dr. Staple chuckled harmlessly. "Somewhat," he answered.

"Well somebody burned Eva to death! You should've heard her screaming in the middle of them flames. It was sad," she said.

"Burned? You mean to tell me that somebody died in there?" Dr. Staple asked in shock.

"Yeah, my girl, Eva. And nobody knows nothing! She didn't bother nobody! She was so nice and laid back. Pretty little thing, but she had a bad habit of messing with bad boys. Couldn't tell her nothing when it came down to them thugs. That's what the streets do to people, suck 'em right in where they can't get out."

Dr. Staple listened, patiently awaiting his opportunity to ask questions.

"Who was in there with her? I mean did the house catch fire with only her inside?" he asked.

"Yeah, she was in there by herself. But the news people said that she was murdered! Say she had been hogtied with razor wire."

Dr. Staple's eyebrows raised in disbelief.

"Are you serious!" he exclaimed, more as a statement than a question.

"Just as serious as that girl getting burned to death," Phyllis countered.

Dr. Staple vaguely remembered Eva, but he did remember her. He again shook his head in pure dismay.

"You said that you live across the street?" he asked.

"For the last three years I have."

"Did you know she had a sister?" he asked

"You know, she mentioned it, I think. It was around the time her mom passed away. But she didn't have a whole lot to say about her. Seemed to me like they had something between them that kept Eva from talking about her. But don't get me to lying, I really can't say she did talk about her."

Dr. Staple sensed something was wrong with this picture. If Siren's sister was her guardian, and her guardian was deceased, then that only left one question. Where was Siren Montago?

"This is a picture of Eva's sister here. Her name is Siren," Dr. Staple explained to Phyllis.

"Damn, she looks just like Eva with them green eyes! But I've never seen her before."

Dr. Lucas felt an instant wave of panic. Maybe Siren was dead somewhere, or being held hostage.

"It was nice meeting you, Phyllis. I have to get going," he said while backpedaling toward his car.

Like an impatient child at Christmas, he fidgeted with his phone trying to dial.

"Hello. Yes... I mean, no, it's not an instant emergency but I need to file a missing person's report for a patient the ward and my office discharged back into society," he told the operator.

"Sir, how long has this patient been missing?" the dispatcher asked.

Dr. Staple fumbled through the file on his lap trying to locate Siren's discharge date. "Six months," he replied.

"And what makes you think your patient is missing?"

"The guardian we discharged her to was murdered!" he yelped.

"What's your patient's name?"

"Siren! Siren Montago..."

Chapter 9

New city, new life…

"Damn! Who is that?" one onlooker asked aloud.

Alexia strutted like the stallion she created herself to be. The Palladium was packed with ladies of all ethnic backgrounds. Siren had never experienced anything close to the attention she was getting as she tagged along behind Alexia. Although the club was a hot spot for the Orlando area, tonight was different. Word had spread that a rapper was going to shoot a scene for is music video at the club. No one actually knew where in the club the scene would be filmed, but certainly the best of the best that the area had to offer were in attendance.

"Alexia?" Heyyy, bitch! Girl, I saw the magazine layout! Girl you look good! They did an excellent job accenting all of your features. Bitchhh, I am so fucking jealous."

Alexia kept her parade smile wide. "Thank you," Alexia sang. "Girl, let me get in this club. I'll talk to you later."

The girl watched Alexia sway off into the crowd. "Crusty ass bitch," she said to Alexia's back.

Not knowing Siren was a part of Alexia's entourage, the woman made the comment right in front of Siren, who found it funny that someone else felt exactly how she felt about Alexia. Without a glance toward the comment, Siren just continued following Alexia.

Within forty-five minutes, the two of them had shuffled into the VIP section. Siren noticed how Alexia was a bottle of freshness. It amazed her because she was exhausted, plus her feet hurt from wearing Alexia's heels. Everything she was experiencing was new to her: the borrowed dress, the borrowed heels, the club, everything!

"What you drinking, girl?" Alexia asked Siren.

Another thing she'd never experienced, alcohol. Siren shrugged her shoulders instead of trying to fight to speak over the loud music. Alexia walked off and before Siren could turn around and survey the VIP area, she was being approached.

"Baby girl, damn! You can't be from around here. Where you from?" the man asked.

Instead of trying to talk, Siren looked into his eyes without blinking. Her bright green eyes bore straight through him. In that instant, his courage began to wither.

"This bitch burnt out," he mumbled as he walked off fully depleted of swag.

"Weak," Siren whispered to herself.

Ever since she was a child, she had been told that her eyes were mesmerizing but this was the first time she'd been able to use them to her advantage.

"Patron Silver and lime," Alexia yelled over the music.

Siren gave Alexia the same look she'd given the guy.

"Bitch, you need to relax! In here staring around like a psych patient with them big green ass eyes! Here, take a few sips of this. Girl, how you gonna meet that meal ticket looking crazy? Follow my lead. Sip your drink through the straw, bat them eyelashes with every sip, and look seductive doing it. Got it? Now come on, crazy girl," Alexia added with a chuckle.

As the night passed, Siren seemed to find comfort in following Alexia's lead. The alcohol had become a tranquilizer. Each sip helped her paranoia to subside. The club lights played in the darkness, making the deep bass of the music feel like a therapeutic session with a masseur. In a trance, Siren slowly gnawed at her lip, sending waves of euphoria through her veins. The moment felt dreamlike.

"Oh my God," she whispered to herself.

"Siren! Girl, are you okay?" Alexia asked with a smirk.

Siren could only nod in agreement as Alexia watched her eyes blink lazily.

"Come on, let's sit down," Alexia said, while tugging Siren's arm.

The two of them plopped down on the couch, seemingly in unison while captured in the same trance.

"I… feel… soooo… good," Siren sang.

"Huh? You say something? I can't hear you over the music."

Siren stared distantly at the people passing by. Her head hung loosely. Alexia smiled at Siren in admiration of her relaxed state.

"You like how you're feeling?" Alexia asked.

With her eyes closed, Siren nodded.

"Welcome to the world of Mollie, the land of good times and great sex!"

Siren shook her head.

"What?" Alexia asked.

"No!" Siren blurted with her eyes still closed. "No!"

"Girl, what in the hell you talking about?"

"Alexia! Damn, baby girl, I thought that was you sliding up in this bitch," a male voice yelled over the music.

Before either siren or Alexia could focus on him, he'd positioned himself between them. The moments were swift for Siren. No sooner than she had the opportunity to recoil from the intruder's presence, she was jerking from someone sitting on the arm of the sofa on her opposite side.

"Ricoooo!" Alexia sang animatedly. "Oh my God, boo, what's up boyyy?"

Rico's chest tilted in an exaggerated posture. Arrogance preceded every word.

"What's up with you?" Rico countered. "Last time I saw you, you were on a mission to get money by any means."

Alexia's eyes bulged a bit. She briefly looked past him at Siren and then back at Rico. The look she gave him made him look over at Siren also. He smiled, showing off a mouth full of gold.

"Who is this?" he playfully asked. "What's up, Red? I'm Rico. What's up with you?"

Siren didn't know what to say. Her mind was still spiraling from the drug Alexia had put in her drink.

"Damn!" Rico yelped. "You a fool with the contacts, like a gotdamn Alaskan Husky in this muthafucka! Aye, Angelo," he called out to the guy who had positioned himself on the arm of the sofa. "Check this lil chick's eyes out."

"I'm hip. Shawty bad as fuck on top of dat," Angelo replied.

Rico bounced his attention between Siren and Alexia before settling on Alexia.

"What y'all getting into tonight?" he asked. "Y'all in here with somebody?"

"Boy, please! You know I don't do the dating life. I'm married to that paper, don't play!" Alexia boasted.

"Paper?" Rico's friend, Angelo, replied. "That's the life right there. I got plenty of dat. You talkin' 'bout this right here?" he asked as he tossed a rubber-banded lump of cash on Alexia's lap.

Not to be outdone, Rico jumped in. "Oh, she know the biz-ni-ee round this piece is official," he added, throwing a bank band of bills on Siren's lap. "This money don't fold," he bragged.

Siren's eyes focused on the bank issued bills. The band told its amount. The largest amount of money she'd ever seen in her life was now lying in her lap. She looked over at Alexia, who was looking back in her direction with a huge smile on her face. Siren didn't know what to say or do so she just returned the goofy smile. Everyone knew what was about to take place, except for Siren. She had no idea that her smile was the official green light that she was down for whatever. A few hours after the agreement, the conclusion of the party had come and the after-party was the topic.

"Alexia, can I speak with you real quick?" Siren asked.

The club lights had come on, signaling it was time to go. Since Rico and Angelo had shown up, Alexia had given her undivided attention to Rico.

"Yeah, girl, what's up?" Alexia asked.

"Are you about to leave with him?" Siren inquired.

Alexia looked around sarcastically. "Uhhh... Siren, girl, it's three in the morning! What else should we be doing?"

"Alexia, I'm not having sex with this guy!" Siren's whisper was firm and unapologetic.

Alexia rolled her eyes in contempt. "Damn, girrrlll," she sang. "You can't see the big picture right now?"

"What picture?"

"Uhhh, hello! Can you say ballin' ass meal ticket?"

Siren shook her head in disagreement.

"What the fuck! Why you acting like a nun and shit? You better let that pussy go, let him bust a quick nut, and get that check outta his ass!" Alexia barked.

They looked away from each other, letting the dispersing club goers be their distraction.

"Well, here, here's the house key. I'll let him drop you off and I'll take Rico with me."

Siren looked at the key. "Why can't you take me, Alexia? I don't want to be alone with this guy!"

Alexia looked Siren over once and dropped the key in Siren's hand.

The ride with Angelo was very uncomfortable. She leaned against the door, trying to focus through the drugs and alcohol.

"How long you staying down here?" Angelo questioned.

"I'm not sure," Siren answered quickly.

"You tryna get something to eat?" he asked.

"No, thank you."

Angelo exhaled his frustration. "Man, what's up with you?" he finally snapped.

"What do you mean?"

"You see a nigga tryna get at you! It's late night and you on some bullshit. What's up?"

She sensed the desperate plea in his voice. "I'm sorry if I made you think that I sell my body for money, but I'm not having sex with anybody. Maybe if you catch up with your friend and Alexia, you probably can pay her."

"Mannn," Angelo sang. Then he turned the music back on and accelerated through the streets.

Siren was relieved that the conversation was over. That was until the car slowed to a stop in front of a residence that she knew was not her temporary home.

"Why are we stopping?" she asked in panic.

"I need to run in and get something. I'll be right back."

Angelo left the car running with his money on the floorboard. Siren just sat there thinking of going to sleep. Five minutes turned into fifteen minutes. Fifteen minutes turned into forty-five minutes. She'd held her pee since leaving the club and couldn't hold it any longer. She looked at the house for activity, yet pure darkness covered the entire setting.

"Damn!" she whispered.

The urgency to use the restroom sent waves through her body. She turned the ignition off and got out of the car. The early morning reeked of piney wetness. She hugged herself as she shuffled up to the door.

"Hello?" she whispered.

The door was cracked open just enough for her to see inside.

"Hello? Angelo?"

No answer echoed back. She nudged the door open.

"Angelo, this is Siren. I need to use the restroom. Hello? Angelo?"

Something screamed in her head to go back to the car, but her body couldn't wait another second. She entered the house and aimlessly found the bathroom. The house was clean but barely furnished. A big screen TV hung on the wall with a Play Station just under it. A couch was the only other furnishing. She finished up in the bathroom and as soon as the door opened, Angelo grabbed her.

"Aahhh! Nooo!" she tried to scream.

"Shhh, calm down! Calm down!" he whispered. "Just listen to what I gotta say."

Siren's breathing was completely out of control even more so when she felt his manhood harden and press against her. He was completely naked.

Chapter 10

Back in the Chi...

An eerie aura filled the space in the car between Derrick and Funk as Derrick slowed to a stop.

"Sixty-seventh and Cottage Grove," Funk stated aloud. "Oakwood Cemetery? Joe, you was serious? Nigga, I ain't going in a cemetery looking for a dead bitch *we* killed!"

Derrick paid him no attention. "Come on," he ordered.

With death lingering over his head like a halo, Derrick knew every option had to be exhausted. Funk trotted behind Derrick like an unwilling participant.

"Damn, Dee! How we supposed to find this bitch when we don't even know her last name? You know how many dead bitches named Eva out here?"

"Gotdamn, nigga!" Derrick growled. "If you let me fuckin' think, shit!"

Funk wanted to express his emotion but knew nothing good would come of it so he began lurking through the aisles of countless headstones.

Hours stacked on top of each other as both of them searched for Eva's gravesite. Exhaustion had taken its toll on Funk. Much more determination rested on Derrick's shoulders.

"Mannn," Funk complained. "This shit crazy! It gotta be an easier way to get this bitch." He looked across the cemetery at his partner, instantly feeling sorry for him. In the midst of his growing sadness for his friend's situation, his phone rang.

"Yeah," he answered.

"Funk?" the caller replied. "This Mitch."

Funk's eyebrows furrowed in confusion. "What's good, fam?" Funk countered.

"You with Derrick?"

"Yeah," Funk answered.

"He lace you up on the business? The message from the top?" Mitch asked.

"Kind of. He put me up on enough of the message," Funk said while watching Derrick from afar.

"Good!" Mitch said. "Because the next time you get a call from me, it'll be for you to close that situation. Alright?"

Funk literally felt his heartbeat in the vein of his neck. Butterflies began performing a ritual dance of uneasiness inside his stomach.

"Me?" Funk inquired nervously.

"Is there something you need to say about it?" Mitch coyly asked. "Maybe a message I need to relay back?"

Funk knew he was teetering on the brink of his own death. "Nooo!" he cried out. "I got this over here."

"Good! Make sure you get it right as soon as you get my call," Mitch replied.

"You know when?" Funk asked.

"As soon as you get my call, fam," Mitch sternly added.

Funk heard the call disconnect. He let his hand freefall from his ear lifelessly. His chin sank into his chest. A fresh bouquet of sympathy flowers stood out in the corner of his eye. As many people as he'd killed and shot at, never had he pictured that those same flowers could be for him for not killing the only true friend he had outside of the gang life.

"Shit," he whispered.

There was nowhere to run and hide. They knew him. They knew his life. They knew his children. The only option left for him was to find this green-eyed bitch. He pinched the bridge of his nose in deep thought.

"Funk! Funk!" Derrick yelled.

Funk looked up from his state of agony to find Derrick frantically waving him over. He ran across the cemetery to where Derrick stood.

"Look!"

Funk followed Derrick's outstretched finger.

"Found that bitch! I found that bitch, Cholly! I told ya!" Derrick excitedly heaved.

Funk couldn't find any comfort in finding the headstone because he was still digesting the fact that he'd been designated to kill the man standing before him at any moment. At that point, time was not on his side. Funk stood next to Derrick, looking down at the small headstone.

"Eva Michelle Montago," Derrick said aloud. "Her sister said her name was Siren. Siren Montago! Siren Montago, I'm coming bitch!"

Chapter 11

"Hello?" Alexia answered.

"Aye, bitch! Where dat hoe at you came to the club wit last night?" Rico barked into the phone.

"Who? What are you talking about, Rico?" Alexia asked while straining to hear.

"The bitch with the green eyes! The bitch that left with Angelo last night! Matter fact, where you at?" he demanded to know.

"Boy, you trippin'! I'm down here at the fairground on day two of Miss Chee's video shoot," Alexia replied.

"That bitch with you?" he asked.

"Yeah, dang. Why?" she cried out.

"I'm on my way!"

Alexia looked at the phone and shook her head. "Where this girl at?" she mumbled to herself.

The fairground was jam packed like it was a concert going on. Luxury cars littered the parking lot as if an exotic car dealership had given them away. Jewelry sparkled under the high beams of the Florida sun, making the all-white linen affair one to remember.

"What this girl done did? I hope she ain't steal something from Angelo! Them Mercy Drive niggas outta control," Alexia mumbled.

After a few minutes, Alexia finally spotted Siren.

"Siren! Siren!" Alexia yelled.

Siren heard her name and looked around with exaggerated expressions on her face until she located Alexia, who was waving her over. Something was definitely wrong and she knew she couldn't waver in giving an explanation. She plastered on her best parade smile as she walked up to Alexia.

"What's up, girlll? It's some real important folks out here. Everybody shining," Siren excitedly stated.

Alexia nodded in agreement and quickly got to the point. Siren, girl, tell me why Rico called my phone screaming and asking where you at? I mean, bitch, he sound mad as hell!"

Siren shook her head in shock. "I don't know what he asking for me for," she said matter-of-factly.

Alexia anxiously sucked her teeth. "Siren, girl, tell me if you stole his money or did something stupid because them niggas is crazy as hell and they don't give a fuck about nobody. So please tell me!"

"I already told you, Alexia, he brought me straight home," Siren whined.

"Okay, bitch, I'm telling you these Florida niggas is crazy! I don't know how they get down up in Chicago, but I know what they'll do down here."

No sooner than the last syllable of her last word could roll off of her tongue, a group of men dressed in black t-shirts and black Dickie shorts with black hats and shoes cut through the all-white affair. Then the commotion began.

"Come on, girl. Let's go see what he want," Alexia stated.

Siren swallowed hard. She made sure her hair was positioned over the bruise on her collarbone. Her heartbeat accelerated the moment Rico pointed her out to his comrades.

"See, I told you something was wrong, bitch," Alexia mumbled through clenched teeth.

"Aye, bitch!" Rico snapped with aggression. "What happened to my partner? What the fuck happened?"

Siren glanced around, seemingly in a daze. "What are you talking about?" she asked.

"Alexia, you better tell this bitch I'm 'bout dat life! Hoe, what happened to Angelo? How the fuck he end up dead? Especially when you was the last one to be seen with him?"

"Dead?" Alexia cut in.

Siren's eyes bulged in shock as Alexia grabbed her chest in panic.

"Is Angelo dead, Rico?" Alexia asked again. "Siren?" she said with a questioning expression on her face.

Siren shook her head frantically in disagreement.

"Uhn-uhn! I… I… Uhn… I… He drove me straight home," Siren pled. She turned her attention toward Alexia and then flinched a moment too late.

"Bitch!" Rico yelled as he followed through with a hard open-handed smack to Siren's face.

Alexia yelped while a bright flash and burning sensation spread across Sirens entire face. She crumbled to the grass in a heap.

"I told you, bitch," Rico threatened standing over Siren.

"Rico!" Alexia yelled. "You is fucking trippin' hitting that damn girl!"

That only enraged him even more. With the extra fuel, he revved up and kicked Siren in the stomach.

"Rico!" Alexia screamed.

"What the fuck happened to my dawg, bitch? And if I have to ask again, I'm shuttin' this bitch down! Now what happened?" he threatened.

"I don't know. But if you don't want it to happen to all you niggas standing here in black, then my muthafuckin' suggestion is that you find your way out the same way you came in!"

Rico looked up to see a dark skinned, stout, bald head, black man who stood at about five feet ten inches staring him directly in his eyes. The stare was eerie and distant, so much so that Rico had to reset by breaking the stare. He looked back at his crew and addressed them instead of the man that was talking to him.

"Who is this nigga? This nigga must don't know who we is," Rico boasted. "Tryin' to save a bitch and shit!"

"First off, let me explain something real quick," the bald man began. His posture was domineering. The blackness in his eyes sat behind lazy eyelids, proving that no excitement was pumping through his veins. His left hand rested in his pocket and his right rested on his abdomen.

"I'm a creator, far from being God, but still a creator. I make, mold, and determine all *my* situations. Therefore, if I would have given a *fuck* about who you were and what you were about, this conversation would have never taken place. You see, power isn't gained by the opponent you beat. It's gained when you warn the opponent of his demise before you beat 'em. Now, the only reason you get this explanation is because this venue is my creation and I won't allow your darkness to ruin my sunshine. It was nice meeting you."

He turned and extended his hand to Siren, who was still sprawled on the grass, embarrassed. Her face stung and her nose bled.

"This is my second time running into you at a GODN venue," the bald man stated. Then he turned around to find himself staring down the crosshairs of Rico's gun.

"Nigga, who the fuck you think you talkin' to like dat?"

A smile crept into the corners of Siren's savior's mouth.

"Take her and both of y'all go join the fun. I'll be around shortly," the man calmly stated.

He stood with his back to Rico until the women had cleared the scene. Then he turned around and noticed that all of the men in black had guns out but Rico was the only one pointing a gun at him.

"My name is Crusher. It doesn't matter whether I was blessed with the name, given the name, or earned the name, the fact remains that my name is Crusher. And now that you know this, the question you need to ask yourself is do you have enough bullets.

The silence was so prevalent that it seemed to actually be loud, as loud as a train's horn. Rico had to force himself to return Crusher's stare.

"I can assure you that the *whole city of Orlando* don't have enough bullets to get within five miles of harming *a piece* of who I am," Crusher added.

Rico started to slowly lower his gun. "That bitch know what happened to my people. She was the last one with him. She know!" he announced.

"Have a blessed day," Crusher softly spoke.

His voice cracked a bit as he said it. His anger had to be restrained because he knew the police was somewhere watching. He had fought extremely hard to be completely legit but he knew that his Chicago roots still ran wild in his heart. He watched as the group backpedaled to their cars.

"I'ma kill that nigga and that bitch! Watch!" Rico vowed to his homeboys.

Crusher walked back to the video shoot. He noticed all of the guns being tucked back under shirts and in the girls' bags. No one bothered to ask him anything. He was livid as he approached Siren and Alexia.

"Thank you!" Siren said.

"Never bring drama to GODN! Never! Am I clear?" he asked. "This is my life! I don't know you and you don't know me. This is a business!" Crusher barked. Without another word, he stormed off, enraged. He just couldn't believe what had just happened.

"Crusher, you good, fam?" his security asked.

"Get my car. And get that green-eyed girl. Something about her is different from these other females. I don't know what it is, but I need to sit down with her and find out.

As clever as he was, he was about to open a door that he would soon wish he would have left sealed.

Chapter 12

"Shit!" Rico moaned while rubbing his nose. He passed the rolled up one hundred dollar bill and a baggie of powder cocaine to one of his goons in the backseat. All of them were high beyond measure. A bottle of Remy followed. The adrenaline from the alcohol and narcotics created a feeling of invincibility for everyone in the car.

Rico drove with a menacing scowl etched across his face. The cocaine would definitely hold responsibility for that. But the electricity of murder that filled his veins came at the thought of Crusher and the green-eyed girl. Touched by mental defeat, Rico felt that he couldn't let life go on without addressing the issue in his own way. They both had to go; no if, ands, buts, or maybes about it! He bit down aggressively. The thought alone sent a chill through him. The conversation replayed over and over in his head. He was livid at how the nigga Crusher had threatened him without actually saying it.

"G.O.D.N," he said aloud.

"Yeah," one of his goons cut in. "Fuck nigga don't know what he just stepped in! This our muthafuckin' city! Nigga ain't even from down here, out-of-town ass niggas!"

The rotation of cocaine had made its way back to Rico. "Hold the wheel," he said while digging into the bag of nose candy. "Yeah," he groaned as the grains of cocaine funneled through his veins. "Yeah!"

His eyelids seemed to be pried open to full capacity.

"Crusher, huh?" Rico grunted. "Kill this pussy nigga!"

The group of highly inebriated goons began getting antsy with anticipation as the car slowed to a stop in front of its destination. The metallic sounds of bullets being chambered echoed over the sounds of snorting cocaine.

"Put that shit up!" Rico barked. "It's time to leave our signature!"

The group filed out of the car donned in their all-black goon attire and masks. Five in total, they all carried short barreled Chinese AK-47s and were led by their leader, Rico. The early morning hour was void of human presence as they walked up the driveway of the home they were about to destroy. Rico stopped at the hood of one of the two cars that occupied the driveway. He felt it.

"These bitches just got home," he mumbled.

His goons said nothing. All they wanted to do was shoot. They really didn't give a damn about anything other than that.

"Kick the door open!"

Upon command, Rico's goons kicked the door and it splintered. All five of them ran in and split in different directions to search the house. Rico grabbed a chair from the kitchen table and sat down. Screams and grunts echoed from the confines of the house. Music played softly. Two of his goons came back empty-handed. The other two came back with two women in tow.

"Look at what we have here," Rico toyed. "I got two bad bitches at the same damn time," he recited from a rap song by 2 Chainz.

His goons forced the two women to their knees just a few feet away from Rico. The women tussled and grunted from being manhandled.

"Where the green-eyed bitch at?" Rico asked.

"Rico," Alexia cried out.

"Hell naw, bitch! Ricooo ain't here to talk! Where is the bitch at?" he countered.

"She left with the cat you were arguing with at the video shoot! She's with him," Alexia whined.

"Rico," one of his goons called out from somewhere in the house. "Bruh, this shit crazy!"

Rico sprang to his feet. "What?" he inquired.

The goon came out of the bedroom with three things in his hands. Two of the three solidified Rico's belief that the green-eyed girl had something to do with his friend's death.

"Look," the goon said.

Rico's eyes bulged from behind his mask. He quickly ripped off the mask. It was his partner's necklace and gun. "She did, she fuckin' killed 'em," Rico growled.

He turned and kicked Alexia's lover in the mouth with the front of his boot. A high-pitch wail christened the room.

"Shut up," he yelled as he racked the assault rifle.

The butt of the gun found the bridge of Alexia's nose.

"Both you bitches lay on your back!" Rico signaled his goons as they all stood over the crying women. The barrels of their assault rifles were trained on the bodies of the two women.

"Rico, please," Alexia cried.

Crusher's words bounced around in Rico's head. His face gritted venomously. "Fuck you, bitch!" he yelled.

Bullets riddled Alexia and her lover recklessly for a full minute. The barrage of gunfire nearly amputated body parts.

"One down, two to go," Rico said as he rolled his mask back down over his face.

Chapter 13

The Chicago Police Department was a normal, everyday wreck. With nearly one hundred thousand arrests per year in the City of Chicago, murder was the leading concern. Any tip was always welcomed. But there was one particularly horrid murder that needed to be solved.

"Lieutenant?" homicide detective Moore called out. "Got something you might wanna see."

"Regarding?" the homicide lieutenant asked in an agitated manner.

"Remember the Montago homicide off of 127th Street?"

The lieutenant looked up from his computer. "The arson homicide?" Lt. Sanders asked.

"That's the one," Moore replied.

"What you got?"

"Well apparently Eva Montago had a sister named Siren Montago."

"And?" Lt. Sanders prodded.

"A missing person's report was called in by a, get this, Dr. Lucas Staple from the psychiatric ward. I followed up the report and found out that this Siren Montago was discharged forty-eight hours before the house fire. And guess who signed Siren out of the ward. Yep, you guessed it, the murdered Eva Montago!"

Lt. Sanders was giving his full attention to Detective Moore now.

"Wait, there's more," the detective continued. "Guess what Siren was admitted for."

Lt. Sanders didn't respond.

"Murder! Evidently, Siren Montago stabbed her father to death when she was fifteen years old. The judge found her incompetent to stand trial and remanded her to the custody of the psych ward for five years. Her mother passed away a little less than three years ago, leaving the only other guardian as Eva Montago."

Lt. Sanders leaned back in his chair, staring blankly at his computer screen.

"And Dr. Staple informed me that Siren's medication prescription was never picked up, nor have her mental disorder checks been cashed. That is what led him to file the missing person's report," Detective Moore added.

"Has the missing report been officially filed?" Lt. Sanders asked.

"Not yet. I wanted to run this by you first," Detective Moore answered.

"Okay, well get it filed and run her picture through the morgue, along with all hospitals and shelters here in the city," Lt. Sanders ordered. "You have a picture of her?"

"Detective Moore tossed the missing report onto his supervisor's desk. Lt. Sanders picked up the file and looked a new person of interest in her bright green eyes.

"Siren Montago," he said aloud.

Chapter 14

"Happy thirteenth birthday, Siren," her dad whispered.

Siren's eyes fluttered open as she woke to see her dad standing over her bed.

"Happy birthday, baby girl," he repeated.

"Thank you, daddy. Where's mommy and Eva?"

"Oh, I had them go run a few errands. It's just me and you," he perversely replied.

Siren was used to his molestation. She knew what it took to get him off so he would leave her alone.

"I have a birthday present for you today. Since you're a teenager now, I think it's time you get to feel what daddy feels. Can I give it to you now?"

Siren nodded, more from fear than anything else. She froze stiff as she watched he dad crawl under her comforter. His slow movements mixed with the unknown had her heart racing. He had never done this before. All she had on was an over-sized t-shirt and some Winnie the Pooh underwear.

She felt his cold fingers tug at her panty line. Then he shimmied her panties off of her. She squeezed her eyes tight in withdrawal as his tongue touched her private.

"Ahhh," Siren screamed as she jolted awake from the nightmare.

"Damn," Crusher said as he drove. "You must've been dreaming about some very serious things."

Siren stared blankly out of the car's window. Her chest heaved nervously. The clock read 4:10am.

"You okay?" he asked.

"Yeah, I'm alright, just had a bad dream. I have 'em on occasion," she assured.

They were just entering into the City of Orlando. They had taken a trip to Daytona Beach. Crusher's reason for going was to calm himself and refrain from unearthing the animal instinct inside of him. Siren agreed to go because she needed some time to figure out an escape from Alexia and the situation she'd created.

"Let me apologize for not talking much. Ummm... I live by the power of the mind so I think everything over in a very meticulous way," he explained. "So don't think I wasn't paying attention to you. It's just that I have a lot on my plate."

"It's okay. I understand," Siren replied.

"So how long you plan on staying here?" he asked.

"I'm not sure. I sure didn't plan on getting beat up," she jokingly replied.

"Speaking of which, if you don't mind me asking, what was that all about anyway?"

"I guess something happened to his friend *after* he dropped me off," she lied.

Crusher showed no interest in her story. By that time, he was pulling up in front of Alexia's home. Siren's attention piqued and Crusher noticed.

"What's wrong?" he asked.

"The door is open! Look!" she panicked.

He looked from side to side for an ambush. The first thing that popped into his head was the altercation at the video shoot. He looked around again in panic himself.

"It don't look like anything is out of the ordinary around here," he comforted. "Maybe she just walked in."

Siren calmed a bit, noticing the other car in the driveway. Crusher noticed the uncertainty in her movements. He cringed because he had no firearm.

"Come on. I got you," he urged.

They both walked cautiously to the door. Crusher had been in the presence of the aftermath of death on several occasions, and the smell in the air was the smell of death, which he knew all too well. He showed no indication of concern. They reached the front door and something was terribly wrong.

"Alexia," Siren's soft voice strained.

No answer.

"Alexia!"

Siren looked at Crusher for conformation. He looked yet again for the ambush. Siren walked inside with Crusher right behind her. Not even ten steps inside he saw her stiffen. Her hand covered her mouth. He knew Alexia was dead.

There was one thing in particular that Siren could identify from the bullet riddled, mangled bodies, and that was Angelo's necklace placed neatly on top of Alexia's body. She immediately panicked. They knew it was her who had killed

Angelo. She ran past the dead bodies and into her room. It had been tossed upside down. She rummaged for the gun she'd shot Angelo with. It was gone!

Siren grabbed the suitcase Alexia's cousin had purchased for her and packed the few things she had. There was one last place she was sure they didn't look. She tore the top of the toilet off and Angelo's money was still there. With her suitcase and the money in hand, she rounded the corner like a bat out of hell.

"Whoa! Whoa! Where you going?" Crusher asked. "You have to stay here and report what you found! You just can't leave like this!"

She panted and looked around. "I can't," she replied.

"Why?" he countered.

"Because it's me they want!" she cried out.

"But why?" he asked.

She just stared him squarely in the eyes and he knew that she was admitting that she'd done what the guy that slapped her said she'd done.

"It's a long story," she finally responded.

Chapter 15

Scouring the big, busy city of Chicago for one lone person was taking its toll on Derrick. Funk followed him for two reasons. One was a demand and the other was merely hope. Each and every time his phone rang, he just knew it was his superior giving him the word. Daily he'd thought about packing up and disappearing. But he couldn't. Things were deeper than that.

"Derrick, man, why you pulling into the hospital? You sick or something?" Funk asked inquisitively.

"Damn Funk, bruh, I've been all over this city looking for this bitch. But I didn't think of checking the hospital."

"What? You losing your mind, Derrick. Remember, the bitch left the hospital."

Derrick looked over at his crony with a look of pure disdain and followed with a shake of his head.

"Come on, man," Derrick somberly said.

The two walked into the hospital with an idea and a hope, split only by their prospective decisions.

"Let me do the talking," Derrick demanded.

The receptionist looked irritated before they made it to the desk.

"Excuse me, miss, but I just flew in from out of town in search of my family member," Derrick explained.

"What's the name?" she asked exasperatedly.

"Siren Montago," he replied.

"Siren? Like a police siren?" she asked with a smirk.

Derrick nodded with a polite smile.

"You sure you have the right hospital? There's no Siren Montago here."

"Oh, I'm sure this is the hospital. Matter of fact, I know this is the right hospital because her accident was on the news. She was in a coma for about six months."

The receptionist's eyebrows knitted in deep thought.

"Ohhh, you talking about Jane Doe, the girl who vanished without a trace," the receptionist replied.

"Yeah! Yeah, that's her," Derrick said with excitement. "You know her?"

"I wouldn't say that. But, again, she ain't here. She vanished," she sassed.

"I know. But what I came to do is speak with the doctor or head nurse who cared for my cousin," Derrick explained.

"And you are?"

"Her only family," Derrick answered.

The receptionist pulled up Siren's medical chart. "Oh okay, the head nurse was Bethany Landon and her assigned doctor was Dr. Roberts."

"Is there any possible way I can have a word with them?" Derrick asked.

"Sure," she answered. "Have a seat and they should be here in a minute."

Derrick and Funk found a place to sit while they both fidgeted nervously. Almost a half hour passed and their nervousness turned into pure anxiety. Derrick couldn't take it anymore.

"Excuse me, miss, it's been thirty minutes and no one has come."

"Have a seat, sir. I assure you they're coming. Trust me."

Her emphasis on the last part of her statement gave him an uneasy feeling. He nodded in agreement without another word.

"Come on, Funk, let's roll," he said in a hushed tone.

Funk could see the urgency in Derrick's brisk walk. He asked no questions as he followed Derrick to the exit. No sooner than they could get their feet onto the concrete, two detectives were exiting an unmarked car. That wasn't what caused sweat to form on Derrick's neck. What did, though, was the clear photograph on a missing person's flyer of Siren Montago!

Derrick and Funk dropped their heads and waited for the detectives to walk inside.

"Run!" Derrick yelped.

The two of them cleared the corner just as the two detectives came running out of the hospital. It was clear that Siren Montago was wanted by more than just them. The million dollar question was *Where is Siren Montago?*

Chapter 16

Crusher sat on the screened-in patio at his hideout condo, which was located forty-five minutes outside of Orlando in a town called Lakeland. The Paddock Club was the name of the high-end development, a nice duck-off right off of the interstate. The patio was ideal because it was screened off with six-foot tall hedges.

The early morning sun beamed down, warming the area by the second. Many times he'd been out there, but this was the one and only time he'd been out there with mixed emotions about a person he knew absolutely nothing about.

Crusher took a deep breath and exhaled through his nose as the sliding glass door slid open, interrupting his solitude. He didn't turn or acknowledge the movement.

"Have you slept any?" Siren asked.

"I can't sleep under these circumstances," he somberly replied.

"I'm sooo sorry these troubles followed me! I really am."

Crusher looked over at her. He couldn't decipher if it was her trancing beauty that had him tolerating her mishaps or if it was just his loneliness. He couldn't quite understand it.

"Who are you?" he asked dryly.

She didn't know if the question was incited by anger or if he actually wanted to know the mind of Siren Montago.

"What you mean?" she dared to ask.

He giggled as though she'd told a joke.

"You know I learned a few things in this life. They say life is a trivial concept, kind of like a puzzle with all the pieces. Some people will get it and others will spend the rest of their lives attempting to get it. I refuse to spend the rest of my life attempting *anything*! I am who I am today because I get it! So please don't insult who I am and what I stand for because I'm finding it hard to understand why you're here. Maybe it's something God is lining up for me, or maybe the devil. But at this moment, I need to know who you really are and not what you want to be!"

Siren looked up at the sky through the screened patio. For the first time since leaving the psych ward, she was at a point in her life where she wanted to tell her story. She got a sympathetic look from the man who had come into her life at uninvited, but at the most needy time of her life. She had no one or nothing in her corner. She'd learned at a very early age that trust meant nothing. While in the ward, she'd memorized the definition of the word *trust*, and at that moment, she had to contradict her entire belief about trust.

"Trust," she said aloud, "assured reliance on the character, ability, strength, or truth of someone or something. Trust, one in which confidence is placed. Trust, a dependence on something in the future or contingent. Trust, hope."

After reciting the definition of the word *trust*, she sat down across from Crusher and began to pour her heart out.

"I was forced to become a cold-blooded murderer at the age of fifteen. I killed the only person a child is expected to put their trust in at that time in their life. I was forced to make a decision at nine years old, a decision that could've destroyed my entire family!" Siren smiled and then countered it with a grunt.

"Humph, it's ironic it happened that way. They're all dead now," she continued.

Crusher didn't want to interrupt by saying anything because he wanted his questions answered.

"But at fifteen, I killed him! I grabbed the biggest knife I could find and stabbed his drunk ass to death! I stabbed him for every fucking time he touched me! I stabbed his ass for every drop of cum he spread all over my undeveloped body! I stabbed the life out of him for making me have orgasms that I was too young to understand! I trusted him! I loved him! He was my daddy! Who do I trust after that?" she questioned.

Tears began to stream from her beautiful green glaciers. Crusher's demeanor remained steady.

"Yes, I killed the guy I was being asked about. Had I not fought for my virginity, I would have been passed around like the rest of the Alexias of the world. I shot 'em in the head with his own gun!"

Crusher watched her tears stream in succession, no huffing, no puffing. He was witnessing a person who hadn't cried since she was a child.

"That's who I am. I'm a murderer," she concluded.

Thoughts ran wild in Crusher's mind. His heart played a tune he was unfamiliar with. Looking at her, his heart told him to help her, but his inner gangster was screaming "fuck this bitch."

"If you want, you can live here while I clean up the mess in Orlando. You're safe here," he said.

"Thank you!" she said, reaching to kiss his cheek.

The warmth inside his body formed a mist of sweat down his back. Now the gangster in him was ready to defend the man his O.G. had raised because forty-five minutes west of where he sat, pure havoc was underway. His phone rang to inform him.

"What's up?" Crusher answered.

"Crusher, where you at? Shit is on fire over here. They killed Tre, Bunk, Pete, and Lil Nez! It's them Mercy Drive niggas."

Chapter 17

The murder of Alexia and her lover was just a light tap of the knockout punch Rico and the Mercy Drive clique had in store. It was about to be a war because of one person. And Rico vowed to kill everything in his way, including the ballin' ass nigga, Crusher. The thought made him snort a nostril full of cocaine.

"Who da fuck these niggas think they playin' wit' out this bitch?" he questioned the plate full of cocaine. "I warned 'em! I warned 'em! Kill one of my muthafuckin' partnas and expect a nigga not to cut up! Got me super fucked up!"

The vibration from his phone buzzed against a table full of guns, clips and bokes of bullets of all calibers. The ravished soul behind the cocaine induced adrenaline rush looked doe-eyed at the phone as though its existence had no purpose. He dug the straw into the pile of cocaine greedily. The phone tried its luck again.

"What, nigga?" Rico barked into the phone. "Blowin' my shit up like a groupie! What?"

"I got the drop on some of that nigga Crusher's people," Damari replied. "They slippin' right now, dawg! What you want me to do?"

Rico listened to one of his goons but couldn't come up with a strategic ambush due to the high energy the drugs were causing.

"Where they at right now?" Rico asked.

"At the car dealership on Orange Blossom Trail," Damari answered.

"Don't let them niggas leave. I'm on my way."

Rico ended the call. Then he vacuumed down another line of cocaine.

"Okay! Okay!" he prodded himself.

He stood and brushed his clothes as if that would help him with his concentration and equilibrium. The demon inside his head continued to chant the same thing over and over. His jaw muscles tightened from the anger. Without another thought, he grabbed two clips, an assault rifle, and Angelo's .40 caliber.

It took him no time to get to Damari. Rico pulled up next to him, and Damari wasted no time jumping into the passenger's seat.

"Them niggas still over there?" Rico asked.

"Yeah, they still there!"

"You got your strap?" Rico inquired.

"You betta believe it," Damari boasted.

"Mask?"

"Yep."

"Good. Grab the duffle bag and we gone touch these pussies in broad daylight," Rico ordered.

Goons on deck was an understatement when it came to the henchmen under Rico. Never had a demand from him been second-guessed by any of them. They were loyal without question and ready to die for Rico all day long. The two got prepared and then took off walking down the busy street as if innocence was all they had to offer.

"That's them niggas right there," Damari excitedly announced.

Cars flew up and down the cluttered business boulevard. Colorful banners and advertisements were hung so closely together that they resembled a makeshift roof.

Rico and Damari walked onto the car lot right past the five gentlemen. Their spirits seemed upbeat until they spotted Rico. Their chatter stopped on a dime.

"Tre, ain't that the nigga from the video shoot?" Dunk asked. "The nigga Crusher had to check?"

"That's him right there! That's him, fam!" Dunk added with enthusiasm.

Rico stopped in mid-stride, dropped the duffle bag, and faced the group.

"I know you niggas know me," he began while sliding his mask down his face. "And now that y'all know, let's finish what we started."

Before the group could comprehend what was about to happen, shots began to ring out in broad daylight. Rico and Damari ducked and grabbed the duffle bag. The shots were coming from Lil Nez, one of Crusher's guys.

"Kenny, get the car," Tre yelled.

Rico and Damari had run into the thicket of cars on the lot as employees of the dealership ran for cover.

"Call the cops! Call the cops!" were the only audible chants in the air. The squealing of rubber against the asphalt could be heard over the panic.

"They gone," Lil Nez yelled.

Kenny came running through the parking lot. An engine revving and tires squealing grabbed all of their attention. In that moment, automatic gunfire erupted. Kenny slammed on brakes as the bodies of his partners dropped unbelievably fast. With no gun, Kenny could only watch as Rico and Damari filled his friends with bullet after bullet.

The wail of police sirens chirped through the massacre. Kenny held his breath when one of the gunmen looked across the car lot toward him. He pointed the assault rifle at him and let off a barrage of rounds before the other gunman insisted that it was time to go.

Kenny didn't know exactly what had taken place after the gun was pointed in his direction. He'd ducked down so far that he was almost kissing the brake pedal the moment bullets began to fly.

A female's screams initiated the beginning of the aftermath. Kenny looked up. Streams of steam bellowed from multiple bullet holes in the radiator. Through the steam, he could see a trail of blood flowing down the hill toward him. Kenny knew what would follow. The citizens of Orlando were about to be introduced to an agony they never knew existed.

Chapter 18

"Carlos, honey, the police are parked outside," Carlos' wife, Shelly, yelled through the house.

Carlos scurried from the confines of his man-cave.

"Shelly, what'd you say?" he questioned.

She had a concerned look on her face.

"It's the cops, baby! They're out front," she replied.

"The cops?" he mumbled. "I wonder what they want."

The doorbell sounded. Carlos hurried to the door to find out what they could possibly want. His heart beat nervously because he had secrets his wife knew nothing about and he hoped that he wasn't about to be forced into a moment of truth. He opened the door.

"Good afternoon, sir," the officer greeted. "I'm Detective Moore and this is Lieutenant Sanders. We're both from the homicide unit. You mind if we have a word with you, sir?"

"Homicide?" Carlos asked, looking at the Chicago PD precinct number stitched onto the detective's shirt. "You mean as in murder?"

Detective Moore nodded in confirmation. "If you will give me a few seconds, sir, I'm sure my explanation will give you a better understanding.

Carlos definitely didn't want his wife hearing that the detectives at the door were from the homicide unit and wanted to question him.

"If you don't mind, can we conduct this business out here? The wife's inside. I really don't want her nervousness on my back."

The two detectives chuckled, fully understanding his position.

"Sir, seven months ago you were in an accident in which you struck a pedestrian on South Fairfield Drive. I'm sure you recall."

"Yes, Jane Doe," Carlos responded.

Detective Moore opened a file. In it, Carlos saw the beautiful Siren.

"This is her, correct?" Detective Moore questioned.

Carlos swallowed hard. "Sir, I would be lying if I told you yes because she was physically destroyed after my truck hit her. But the skin complexion is about exact," Carlos lied.

"Well we're here to assure you that this is the woman that was hospitalized from that vehicular injury. You are Carlos Boatwright?"

Carlos nodded.

"This woman's name is Siren Montago. Now, the reason we're here is because Siren was released from the psychiatric ward for murder and within forty-eight hours of her release, her sister had been murdered and Siren was in a coma. Following all of that, Ms. Montago (Siren) came out of her coma and vanished the same day. We have strong reasons to believe that one of two things happened. Therefore, either she's in danger, or she is the danger. Either way, Mr.

Boatwright, we need to know if, by chance, you've had any contact with Ms. Montago at all," Detective Moore explained.

At that moment, the front door of the house opened with urgency.

"Carlos, honey, your aunt from Florida is on the phone. She sounds hysterical," his wife announced.

"Babe, tell her I'll call her back as soon as I'm done here," he replied.

"I will. But is everything okay out here?" she inquired with concern in her voice.

"Everything's fine. The officers just had a few questions about the accident," he answered. "I'll be in shortly, babe."

He turned his attention back to the officers.

"Told ya. She's very inquisitive, very!" Carlos added with a smile. "But as far as seeing the girl, no, I haven't."

The officers looked at each other, something they did to make people nervous.

"Well if, by chance, she contacts you, could you please give us a call down at the precinct? Here's my card," Detective Moore added.

"I definitely will," Carlos agreed. "You men have a blessed day."

The officers turned to leave.

"Excuse me," Carlos called out as they walked toward their car. "If you guys don't mind me asking, you said she was admitted to the psych ward for murder, who'd she kill?"

"Her dad," Detective Moore replied.

"Her dad?" Carlos probed.

"Her dad!" both officers repeated in unison.

Carlos couldn't believe what he was hearing. He knew about her sister dying but he didn't know that she was a murderer. He shook his head as he walked back inside. His wife stood with her arms crossed awaiting an explanation.

"What was that all about?" she asked, getting straight to the point.

"Jane Doe, the woman I hit, has somehow vanished from the hospital and they wanted to know if, by chance, I'd heard from her."

"Oh, well you might need to hurry and call your aunt. She insisted that you call her ASAP."

Carlos nonchalantly dialed his aunt's number while looking down at the detective's card.

"Heyyy, Aunt Janice. How's every…" He couldn't finish his greeting before she cut him off. His aunt crammed a bundle of words together, forming a sentence that made no sense to him.

"Wait! Wait! Hold up, Aunt Janice! Slow down. I can't understand you. What'd you say?" he prodded.

He listened and each word she said trampled his heart.

"They killed her? Who killed her? Aunt Janice, I'm not understanding!"

Carlos' wife had closed the gap between them and was now standing directly in front of him. He could only listen as the bad news stomped on his chest. After ten long minutes, his aunt had finally worn herself out with all the crying and explaining. He informed her that he would be down there soon before disconnecting the call.

"What happened, honey?" his wife asked.

"My little cousin, Alexia, was found shot to death in her home," he somberly replied.

"Oh my God, Carlos," his wife whimpered.

After what the detective had just said about Siren Montago murdering her own dad, the only thought on Carlos' mind was that he'd sent a murderer to live with the family member that was now in the same place as the murderer's dad. His guilty conscience could only scream *Siren Montago*.

Chapter 19

Davenport, Florida was thirty minutes outside of GODN's headquarters. It was an emergency meeting spot for situations like this. However, this was the first time Crusher had to assemble a meeting of such dire urgency.

Crusher pulled into the vacant plaza. He'd purchased the whole lot where the plaza sat upon settling in Orlando. From the outside, no one could tell if people were inside, but he knew the difference.

A deep exhale of disbelief escaped his chest. Thoughts of the life he'd given up were painful. But he'd made the decisions that had to be made to avoid a gangster's demise, his demise.

He got out and made his way to the emergency exit door, which was located on the side of the building. The door opened before he even got close enough to knock. The commotion inside was very intense.

"Everybody is here," the doorman said.

Crusher said nothing. The first person spotted him and, like a domino effect, the chatter simmered down to complete silence. One thing everyone knew was that it was imperative that they gave their boss their undivided attention.

"Alright, check this out. All activities are suspended! Shows, photo shoots, club appearances, going out, shopping, everything! I need all of my people to evacuate the City of Orlando within three hours after we leave here today! I would rather everyone relocate to Atlanta until *I* deem it safe to resume the entertainment business. You all know what to do while in Atlanta, nothing illegal and nothing that'll tarnish or stain our brand. Am I clear thus far?"

"What about Lil Nez, Pete…"

"I said," Crusher interrupted, "you have three hours to clear the city! Those who know what's next can stay put. All others, I'll see everybody in Atlanta. Be careful," he stated in closing.

Crusher stood while his employees filed out, eager to follow his directions. Those who remained had to remove their phony exteriors and reveal themselves.

"I hate to do this but we have to revert back to our roots. I'm sure I don't have to explain. Brendon, take that flight. Tell Mitch I need 'em. Explain only what happened to Lil Nez and them, nothing more. Send everybody back on Greyhound buses, trains, and charters. Lance, go pay all of our utilities for the next ninety days. Everything under the company's name should be paid, alright?"

Lance nodded.

"Frank, make sure we have enough pre-paid lawyers, just in case somebody goes to jail. We need direct lines of contact to them after payment. Hell, we probably won't need 'em, but it's always better to have them than not to. Tobias, fam, get in touch with Lil Nez's people, Pete's people, Dunk's people, and Tre's people. Let them know that they're insured under a policy at GODN and all funeral costs will be paid for. Also, let them know that whatever they chose for their funeral is backed by GODN Entertainment 100%!"

Silence filled the room.

"Am I missing anything?" Crusher mumbled aloud.

No one said a thing.

"We're about to turn Mercy Drive into the property of GODN! I'm sick of playing games. Plus, you already know, when it comes to harming family, there is no understanding. Now let's get this done quickly. Brendon, when the guys get here, make sure to camouflage their arrival. And don't let any of them go to Orlando!"

Crusher looked into the eyes of each man.

"We good?" he asked.

They all seemed to be on one accord.

"Let's get outta here!"

"BOS, can I speak with you real quick?" Tobias asked.

Crusher nodded to the others, signaling their dismissal.

"What's up, Tobias?"

"I don't want you to take no disrespect when I ask you this. But I'll be frank about it," Tobias began, trying to work up enough courage to finish his thought.

Crusher stopped, put his hands in his pockets, and focused on the tile floor, giving Tobias his undivided attention.

"You know I watch everything, that's my job. And since we relocated from Chicago down to Orlando, things have been unbelievably profitable. All of our dealings are super legit. Our brand has grown beyond belief. We're breaking through every barrier of each branch of entertainment. I remember when this was only a mere blueprint. Now we are the conglomeration of success!" Tobias explained.

Crusher couldn't get any sense of the direction the conversation was heading. He could only listen. Tobias mentally fought to find the proper words.

"Crusher, bruh, none of this shit started until that girl you saved at Chee's video shoot came along."

Crusher's eyebrows knitted in offense. Tobias noticed the change in Crusher's demeanor.

"I'm just saying, like, who is this bitch?" Tobias quickly added with his palms in the air in a defenseless motion. "She comes out of the blue, gets the shit slapped outta her, you step in and dismiss the nigga, and bam C-4 is about to explode!"

Crusher's eyes narrowed as he smoothed his hand over his neatly trimmed goatee.

"I sense the implication now," Crusher calmly began. "You're trying to tell me in a brotherly fashion that… that all this is about to take place because I saved the woman who was slapped. Am I understanding correctly?"

"Uhhh… Basically, bro," Tobias gave in.

"And you're assuming what? That there's some sort of possibility that I can get this squashed? "

"No! No! Hell no! I wouldn't want to squash this if I could myself," Tobias corrected.

"Then what is it you're saying, Tobias?"

"Don't let that bitch be the reason everything is destroyed. No disrespect!" Tobias quickly added.

"In all the years you've known me, when have you ever known a female that's altered my lifestyle? When?" Crusher barked. "Always business first! A bitch will never be the reason I fall. Divided we fall, united we stand!" he chanted.

They shared a look of assurance that words could never express.

Chapter 20

The community setting in the Paddock Club was upper-class. The cars in the parking lots were unmistakably those of CEOs and prominent business people. Siren seemed to be living a dream. Recalling the events she'd endured to get to this point, she could only rub her temples for relief. The question she needed an answer for seemed to be the culprit behind the built-up stress. She exhaled in defeat, which was all she could do at that point.

"Come on, girl. Snap out of it!" she told herself aloud.

She slapped her palms against her thighs in frustration as she looked around the enormous bachelor pad. She decided the kitchen would be a good place to try to take her mind off of things. She walked into the kitchen and began rummaging.

"Damn! What does he eat?" she questioned the bare refrigerator. A bottle of red wine was just about the only thing in it. She stared at the bottle with some hesitation but her stress level forced her hand to reach for it.

"What are you doing, Siren?" she asked herself.

After grabbing a glass from the dishwasher, she poured the wine into the glass, shrugged her shoulders, and took a long sip.

"Umph! Ahh!" She recoiled from the taste.

The next sip tasted a bit milder than the first. A smile crossed her lips as the warmth of the wine made its way through her body. Her eyes bounced from the bottle to the cup, trying to determine her limit.

"Oh well," she shrugged as she refilled the half-full glass.

She sauntered over to the stereo system mounted to the wall and searched for the button to turn it on. After pressing almost all of them, she laughed aloud when she found the right one.

"It says power," she said in a giddy nature.

Music poured from the hidden speakers. She wasn't familiar with the song so she looked at the display.

"Tyrese, *I Can't Go On*," she read.

She stepped back and took a sip of the wine as she listened. The song was near the end and soon faded out. The next song began to play. Instantly, upon hearing the beat, Siren knew it was Chicago's very own, R. Kelly. She raised the glass and her free hand in salute to the hometown R&B king. He was her mother's favorite artist. She mimicked how her mom used to dance when R. Kelly songs came on. The slow winding motion seemed to soothe her stress level.

"It seems like you're ready. Girl, are you ready?" she sang.

After another sip of the wine, Siren was feeling good. She sat the cup down, grabbed a pillow, and pretended it was her dance partner. She two-stepped happily until one R. Kelly song faded and another one came on. She stopped moving. Her heartbeat seemed to speed up. Moisture glazed over her eyes as the song played. She had been victimized for the first time to this song. She hurriedly skipped over the song.

"No, Siren! No tears! No!" she demanded herself.

She jumped back in fright as the front door opened.

"My God! You scared me half to death!" she panted

Crusher smiled. "If I remember correctly, this is my condo, right?" he cheerfully joked.

Siren grabbed the glass and took a long swig. "I hope you don't mind, but I rummaged through the kitchen and found a bottle of wine," she said.

"Hold up! Hold up! You mean to tell me you drinking my wine *and* playing with my music?" he asked with a smile. "That's the worst thing you could have done! See, I don't know if this is gonna work."

Siren blushed as she smiled. "There is absolutely nothing to eat in here. You left me here like that!" she said with a frown.

"It's some Cup-o-Noodles in there."

"Really?" she sassed.

"What? I was raised on them things."

"Crusher," she sang.

"Alright, Alright! I'm kind of hungry myself," he said. "Thing is, we gotta order in."

"Order in? Why? What happened?"

"Siren, the questions," he replied while shaking his head. "I'll go out and get all the things we need. But for now, it's just you and I, pretty lady."

Siren finished up the rest of the wine in her glass. "Anymore?" she asked raising the glass.

They shared a laugh. They both knew that the laughter was more from nervousness than actual comedy. To avoid the inevitable awkwardness that would follow the nervous laughter, Crusher picked up the phone to order their food and Siren went off to take a shower.

There was obviously an attraction growing between the two of them but they were both in denial, trying their best to ignore any emotion that threatened to interfere with their business. Eventually, reality would set in for the both of them.

"Siren?" Crusher called out. "The food has arrived."

She cut the shower off. "Huh?" she yelled as loud as her soft voice would allow.

"The food is here," he repeated.

"Okay," she replied as she turned the shower back on.

Trying to refrain from being romantic, he grabbed his food out of the bag and sat hers inside the microwave.

"She can fix her own food," he mumbled, reassuring himself that he was in control.

He'd admitted to himself that she was extremely beautiful. There was no denying that. But Tobias was right, there was no way he could let her step in out of the blue and settle down. It just couldn't happen.

"Ugh," he heard her sigh from behind him.

The smell of shampoo and lotion met his nose before he could turn around. He unwillingly inhaled the scent. As many women as he'd fucked and discarded, he just couldn't understand what was so different about this woman. Something must have been wrong with his *Fuck a Bitch* card, he figured.

"That's how you treat a guest? Oh, okay. Now I get it. I'm a hostage, that's why," she added while nudging his shoulder.

"What?" he asked.

He turned around to a sight of plain sexiness. She had her hair wrapped in a towel turban. The wife beater hugged her slender body to perfection. Her small breasts stood up without effort. Her nipples were slightly hard from the cool air. The plaid boxer shorts were plain but the way she rolled the elastic band down cause the boxers to hug her crouch area. He quickly noted all these attributes in one nervous scan.

"Eating without me, that's what," she pouted, following his eyes quicker than he could realize.

He was caught. He laughed it off and reverted back to the food subject.

"I told you I was hungry," he said while scooting past her.

As he passed her, he closed his eyes tight and tried to think of something trivial but his dick seemed to be on auto-pilot.

"The food is in the microwave, hostage," he teased.

The two of them ate their food with very little conversation. But the one thing Crusher noticed was that her nipples hadn't taken a break yet. Then it dawned on him, it must have been the wine.

"So do I have to go get some more wine?" she asked. "You said you had more."

"You found that, didn't you?" he laughed.

Siren got up and walked into the kitchen. Crusher bit down on his bottom lip as he watched her petite ass jiggle with each step.

"I can't find it," she sang.

He happily got up to assist her. "It's in the walk-in. Come on, let me show you," he said.

"Damn! What are you? Some kind of connoisseur or something?" she asked, squeezing past him.

"Hold up! Don't just be grabbing shit. This is my good stuff!"

"So what was I drinking then?" she asked.

"Grocery store wine," he said in a burst of laughter.

After letting his joke settle for a moment, he said, "I'm just bullshitting."

"I wanna drink this," she said, grabbing a gold bottle.

Crusher reached over her shoulder and grabbed the base of the bottle. The both froze for a moment, which seemed more like an hour to them.

"Not his one, it's for special occasions."

She let it go but didn't move. He slid the bottle back onto the shelf. When he stepped forward, she stepped back into his chest. He quickly looked at her and then tried to return his gaze to the wine. But she spun around in front of him and kissed his lips softly. He tried to back away but she rested her hands on both sides of his face.

"I want to give you something I've been holding onto my whole life," she whispered.

For the first time in his dangerous life, Crusher's heart began to flutter. Siren's bright green eyes locked on his dark lifeless eyes.

"I don't want to die without giving myself to someone I think is worthy of it," she explained.

"What makes you…" he started to ask before she cut him off.

"Shhh!" she hissed while placing two of her fingers over his lips. "Please, make love to me. Please." She turned and grabbed the gold bottle. "That makes this a special occasion," she added while letting her hand trail from his lips to his belt buckle.

Crusher managed to mumble the one word that could describe the good and bad that would come out of his current situation as he was tugged by his belt, "Fuck!"

Chapter 21

"This is our city! We ain't lettin' nothin' set up shop down here!" Rico growled, addressing his crew of goons. "We gon' knock niggas heads off 'round here! Ain't no more fakin'! We ain't stoppin' until we get that bitch with the green eyes! I'm a put a bullet from Angelo's gun right in between them pretty green eyes!"

"Aye, Rico, you know the nigga that saved that bitch? He own the magazine building off Colonial. We can probably catch him over there. You tryna go see?" one of his goons asked.

Rico pulled heavily on his blunt, which was laced with cocaine. The aroma was a favorite amongst the crew. He had no problems putting it in rotation, as the next man greedily grabbed it from him.

"Am I tryna go? Nigga, I oughta blaze your ass up for askin' me some dumb ass shit like dat there," Rico snapped. "Let's get deep and go see 'bout this nigga!"

It took them no time to mount up in three cars and trail each other to one of the GODN offices. The city was in pure shock from the extreme amount of murders that had taken place in such a short period of time. The news stations etched a vivid account of every murder into the minds of everyone who had a TV. The police beefed up patrol, assuring the touristic city that they had complete control. But the truth was that they were just as lost as GODN's secretary, Shannon, was.

She was in the office finishing up a few things before heading out to Atlanta. She was almost done when the automated voice chimed in over the soft jazz that was playing.

"You have visitors," the doorbell sounded.

She looked up at the locked tinted glass doors. "We're closed," she yelled.

"I can't hear you," Rico yelled, signaling with his hands.

Shannon reached for the automatic door opener. At the same moment, the phone rang. She held up a finger to the man outside, signaling for him to wait a second.

"Gentlemen of Distinguished Nature," Shannon said into the phone.

"Shannon," Tobias yelled. "What the fuck you doing at the office? You were told to get the fuck out of Orlando! What are you doing?" he seethed.

She didn't know what to say.

"Fuck!" he yelled. "Did anybody follow you?"

"I don't know, Tobias," she finally answered. "There's somebody at the door right now though."

"What?" Tobias panicked. "What he look like?"

"Kind of tall, thick dreadlocks, and…"

"Gold teeth," they said in unison.

"Tobias, they got guns," she screamed.

"Run! Run, Shannon! Run out the back," Tobias yelled.

"Tear this bitch down," Rico ordered.

Five of his goons opened fire on the front of the building with automatic guns. Shannon ran like a gazelle, especially when the bullets started pelting the glass door.

"Get that bitch," she heard someone yell.

She burst into the Florida sun from the fire exit in full panic. She ran as fast as her little legs would carry her. Luckily for her, a police cruiser was parked on the side of the building next to the one she'd just escaped. She watched the officer frantically grab the door handle to get out. Automatic gunfire littered the whole windshield of the cruiser. Shannon skidded to a stop on her face as she tripped over her tired legs.

"Please," she cried.

She just knew it was over. Her life was over at twenty-seven years old. She lay there cradling her bleeding face.

"Are you hit? Have you been shot, ma'am?" the officer called out.

Shannon thought she was dreaming.

"Ma'am?" he called out. "Twelve-twenty-one to dispatch, shots fire at an officer! I repeat, shots fired from assault weapons!"

"What's your location twelve-twenty-one?" the dispatcher asked frantically.

"East Colonial Drive, behind the magazine company GODN!"

"Ten-four, assistance is in route!"

"Ma'am?" the officer called out to Shannon.

Chapter 22

Siren had finally found an outlet for the pent up frustrations of life. Never had she felt any sensation that felt as good as the sensations she was currently experiencing. Heavy panting escaped the chests of the two giddy love-makers as Siren lay flat on her stomach while Crusher straddled the back of her legs. He'd just experienced his second orgasm of the night.

Only once before in his life had a woman claimed he was her first. But after being with Siren, he automatically knew the first woman had lied about being a virgin. He panted in disbelief at how fast each nut had come. He looked at the glaze of wetness that covered his manhood. He could only close his eyes and bask in mental bliss.

He gently began to sensually massage the back of Siren's thighs, slowly moving up to her back and arms. Siren moaned as his strong hands gripped her neck in a soothing kneading motion.

"Ummm, that feels so good," she crooned.

His fingers trailed behind her ears and then slowly to her scalp. The more she groaned, the more his manhood seemed to revive itself. Once it was at full attention again, he could no longer resist the urge. He stretched out on top of her back. With his hands holding his weight, he arched his back and moved around until the head of his manhood found the mouth of her love nest. He slowly pushed forward and the warmth of her insides burst through the tip of his shaft.

Siren grabbed his wrist for leverage. Crusher gritted his teeth as the walls of her insides contracted around his shaft.

"Ooohhh, Crusher," she whispered. "Ooohhh," she gasped.

He felt the tremble through her grip. "Relax," he mumbled. "I'll be gentle."

He pushed all of him inside of her. Instead of pulling out, he short stroked in a gyrating circular motion. The smell of her hair funneled an array of sensations through his mind. The many women who'd been under his spell flashed through his mind. Never had he believed in love, love at first sight, or even the mere possibility of trying love out for a test run. His lifestyle didn't allow him to trust love. He'd learned that love and loyalty were totally different concepts but it was loyalty that had built the empire he was overseeing. The more he revisited his past, the harder his thrusts became.

"Ahhh! Ohhh! Oh shit!" Siren cried out. "Yes!" She hissed.

Her back dipped as she lifted her ass higher so he could dig deeper. "Yes! Ohhh yes! Don't stop! Don't… Don't stop, baby," she groaned.

He pulled out of her and flipped her onto her back. That one move changed the passion level from moderate to extreme.

"I never felt like this before," Siren muttered.

The cool air attacked the wetness covering his manhood. He grabbed both her ankles, shifting both of them in one hand. He leaned them across his right shoulder and used his free hand to guide his dick back inside of her.

"Uhhh," they both moaned.

He wrapped his free hand around her legs, which gave him leverage to go deeper. After a few thrusts, he pulled her to the edge of the bed and stood up, maintaining the same position. He dove in and out, pounding every inch of his dick into her.

"Ohhh! Oh! Oh! Ahhh," she moaned.

He grunted ferociously. They looked into each other's eyes. His chest heaved in short spurts and he began pumping as fast as he could.

"Ooowww, I'm 'bout to nut again," he mumbled.

"Kiss me," she demanded.

He threw her legs open and began to thrust uncontrollably. She wrapped her legs around his waist and her arms around his neck as their tongues fought passionately.

"I'm about... I'm about to... Ohhh, Crusher!"

He felt the texture of her insides thicken to a more silky smooth sensation.

"Damn!" he grunted.

He then scooped her up, put her back against the wall, cupped her ass in his hands, and went to work. After no more than a few pumps, he was shuddering like a wet puppy.

"Gotdamn, Siren," he groaned as his cum streamed inside of her in quick succession. "Damn," he huffed.

She kissed him all over his face. Instead of pulling out, he sat on the edge of the bed with her on his lap.

"You're an animal, girl," he panted.

She rocked back and forth on his dick.

"You created this animal," she replied while pushing him back on the bed.

Chapter 23

"Fuck! This bitch! It's crazy that these niggas gonna kill me for this shit! I don't know where this dumb ass hoe at," Derrick fumed.

Although females were walking around half naked in the strip club where he sat, his mind wouldn't allow him to focus on that. He shook his head in defeat. In his mind, he had such a clear picture of the battered girl. She looked to be a monster from the swamp. Those piercing green eyes looked like they held a locker of secrets. Again, he shook his head.

"Hmph," he chuckled aloud at the memory.

Then he thought about his partner, Funk, who was a real nigga to him. He could've easily fallen by the wayside while all of this played out. But Derrick clearly saw that, outside of their organization, Funk was the one he could truly depend on through it all.

"Hey, babe, you want a dance?" a stripper asked him.

"Naw, I'm good, fam," he earnestly replied.

"How the fuck am I gonna get outta this?" he silently questioned.

His attention was focused on thoughts of his life when his phone rattled on the table. The call was coming from his superior.

"Yo," he answered, briskly exiting the club so he could hear.

"I need to see you," Mitch calmly stated.

"I'm on trying to get her, fam," Derrick pled, assuming that was his superior's only reason for calling.

"I need to see you, Cholly," Mitch demanded.

"Right now?" Derrick nervously asked.

"If I didn't need you now, then why would I be calling now?" Mitch sarcastically asked.

"I'm on my way," Derrick replied.

The call ended and Derrick stood outside the club, thinking that his time had just expired. His thoughts gave him the urge to get a few more drinks and some quick pussy. He turned to go back inside but saw Funk walking toward him with a glare in his eyes. Derrick had never seen him look like that before.

"What's up?" Derrick asked.

"You ready?" Funk countered.

Derrick knew at that instant that Funk had received the same call; at least he hoped it was the same call.

"Shit gotta be important for him to call both of us," Derrick prodded.

Funk ignored the comment and they walked to the car in complete silence. Being a gangster had its perks, Derrick thought, but he was seeing that being a *fuck up* wasn't to be tolerated.

"What's up, Funk? Joe, you act like something wrong. You good?" Derrick asked.

"Dee, man, let's just see what fam want. I got kids and shit. I mean…"

Derrick knew enough about being a street soldier to know that explanations weren't a part of their lifestyle.

"I feel you, fam," Derrick sadly replied.

The car ride for Derrick was like driving to his own funeral, thirty-five long, agonizing, fear-filled minutes, no music, just two men alone with their thoughts. One thinking of how quickly he wanted to die and the other thinking about murking his crony and being promoted for his dirty work.

When they finally reached their destination, both Derrick and Funk sat up in their seats as the same thought crossed both their minds, *This may be a casket party for the both of us.*

"Shit!" Funk yelped for the both of them.

Once inside, Derrick saw a few people he'd never seen before were there. He looked at Funk for confirmation. Funk simply shrugged. He had no idea what was going on.

About twenty minutes later, once everyone had arrived, the meeting began.

"There's a big problem that we have to handle immediately," Mitch began. "We have a message that came down from the top. Aye, Brendon, go ahead and lace them on the details of the message."

Brendon stood in the circle and explained the message. Everybody's mouth fell open in disbelief. They had only heard rumors about Crusher's status and bloody past. The vision they'd put together to match what they had heard about

Crusher was in the likes of Lou Ferrigno. By the end of the messenger's spiel, their faces had gone from shock, to gritty anticipation, to blatant eagerness at the thought of carrying out this once in a lifetime opportunity.

The citizens of Orlando really didn't know what was about to happen to them. The Mercy Drive crew would definitely regret bringing their enemies from the city of bullets to the city of tourists.

The meeting dispersed and the crowd set out to round up their troops.

"Derrick," Mitch called out. "Let me speak with you real quick."

Derrick quickly stepped over to Mitch. "What's good?" he asked.

"This is your only pass. But when you get to Florida, I want you to explain your situation to the *old man*. Don't leave nothing out! And you'll get to see what he thinks about someone killing one of his people."

Derrick swallowed hard.

"Go get ready to go. Hopefully, I'll see you when you get back. Tell Funk to come here," Mitch finished.

A quick glance at Mitch's eyes let Derrick know the reality of letting the green-eyed girl get away.

"What's up?" Funk asked Mitch.

"After he meets with the *old man*, make sure you see to it that he dies in Orlando with the rest of them niggas down there!"

Funk nodded. He felt bad that one bitch could destroy a real nigga.

Chapter 24

"Make sure your teeth don't scrape the skin," Crusher instructed.

"What? Like this?" Siren replied.

This was the first time she'd willingly given oral sex to someone. But by the way Crusher was gripping the sheets, she figured she must've been doing everything as instructed.

"God! Oh-oh-oh! Damn!" he stuttered. "Suck that dick! Ohhh shit!"

As he watched her mouth glaze his dick, she sporadically looked up with those captivating eyes and moaned with his dick halfway down her throat. It was their third day of nonstop sexing. The only time they even attempted to come up for air was to eat. He couldn't believe he'd cum as many times as he had without losing interest. Her beauty was so heartwarming that it was becoming eerie.

"Damn! That shit feels good as fuck!"

A sharp knock on the front door made him jolt in panic, which caused his dick to accidentally rake across Siren's teeth.

"Gotdamn! Oh shit!" he cried, cradling his dick like an injured child.

"Oh, baby, are you okay?" Siren curiously asked.

"Hell naw! That shit hurt like a bitch!"

The brisk knocking seemed to be a bit harder with each rap. Through the mental fog caused by their daily love making, it didn't dawn on him that he was at his honeycomb hideout.

"Baby? You didn't order anything, did you?"

The heavy knocking persisted and Crusher panicked.

"Shit!" he barked.

He jumped off of the bed with urgency and bolted to the refrigerator, grabbing his gun from behind the panel. The knocking turned to banging. Crusher chambered a bullet into the nose of the .45 automatic. Siren froze. She stood in the bedroom doorway wrapped in the comforter from the bed. Crusher looked through the peephole. He saw the one and only person who knew about his spot. He glanced over his shoulder at Siren.

"Fuck!" he mumbled to himself as he opened the door.

Tobias ran in with a gun in his hand.

"Damn, Cee! Man, you had me thinking the worst! Bruh, I been calling you and calling and calling! Bruh, the office got…" he paused mid-sentence. His attention had been captured by something that was totally unexpected. He couldn't believe what he was seeing.

Crusher could see the disbelief etched on Tobias' face. Tobias looked back and forth between the two of them. He knew better than to question Crusher but he so badly wanted to say just one thing to his superior.

"What's up, Tobias?" Crusher prodded. "What's so important?"

Tobias looked at Siren. Crusher knew what he was insinuating.

"It's good. What's up?" Crusher said, basically giving Tobias permission to talk in front of Siren.

"They shot up the office and almost killed Shannon! They shot up a police car too!"

"Shannon? What was she doing at the building after the notice was given? I don't understand," Crusher barked.

Tobias' energy level had decimated to a pout-like demeanor. "I don't know, mannn! I asked her the same shit," he whined.

"And," Crusher yelled. "What was her excuse?"

"Said she had to tie up some loose ends," Tobias replied.

Crusher exhaled more from his order not being followed rather than the building being shot up.

"Gotdamn, Tobias! You trying to find me, nigga, you need to be making sure GODN is out the way. I don't need the police thinking we in a war with anybody! Gotdamn, Tobias!"

The anger Crusher was spewing really had nothing to do with Tobias. It was because of the talk he and Tobias had shared about the very person standing in the doorway. He buried his head in his palms. All three of them stood in awkward silence. Siren didn't know Tobias. But Tobias had developed instant hatred for her.

"I'm sorry, bro! I lost my footing. Everything is under control. Shannon is gone to Atlanta now. Her face is skinned up pretty badly from running and falling. I only came here because your safety is my main priority. Again, my bad," Tobias said with sadness.

"Don't act like that, Tobias! We don't breed that kind of shit and you know it," Crusher scolded.

They both knew he was speaking of Tobias' somber demeanor. Tobias didn't respond. He simply tucked his gun back into his waistband and walked out. Once the door shut behind him, Tobias stood there for a moment trying to figure out why Crusher wasn't seeing how this green-eyed devil was the cause of everything that was going on. He just felt she was the culprit.

"Divided we fall, united we stand," he recited, remembering Crusher's own mantra.

Crusher stood on the inside of the door tapping his gun against his leg. He plopped down on the sofa and placed the handgun on the glass table. Again, he dropped his head into his hands. Siren didn't know she was the elephant in the room. And although Crusher knew he should have been trying to distance himself, the bold reality of it was that her innocence had hooked a chunk of his heart that *he* didn't even know existed.

Her soft hands cradled the back of his head as she stood over him. He grabbed the back of her legs and buried the crown of his head into her abdomen.

"Baby?" she called out in a whisper. "Let me kill him. I'm who they want."

Crusher looked up and their eyes met. She returned his intense stare.

Chapter 25

"Lieutenant Sanders?" Detective Moore called out while tapping lightly on his office door.

"What's up, detective? Come on in."

"Sir, I know you're busy and I hate coming in here on a hunch, but, if you don't mind, I would like to throw a quick theory at you about the Carlos Boatwright guy we went and talked to."

Lieutenant Sanders leaned back in his chair and crossed his hands over his stomach.

"I'm all ears, what you got?" the lieutenant replied.

"I did more background work on the vanishing of Siren Montago and it stemmed from Mr. Boatwright's answers to our questions."

"I don't understand, detective. I didn't get anything fishy from his answers."

"But I did. See, when we mentioned that she'd vanished from the hospital, he showed no interest in the woman he put in the hospital. There was an abundance of things that just weren't adding up. One was that the nurse reported that only two people had shown any concern for Siren while she was in a coma. One never left a name, but Mr. Boatwright called weekly, and sent cards and flowers. He was deeply concerned. Now the nurse told me that the moment Ms. Montago vanished, both callers stopped calling and Mr. Boatwright stopped sending his sympathy. No biggie, right?"

Lieutenant Sanders shrugged nonchalantly.

"No biggie," Detective Moore stated matter-of-factly. "Now when we asked Mr. Boatwright if we could come in to discuss the victim's demise, he got skittish like he'd been sleeping with Ms. Montago rather than being the person who'd nearly killed her. So I pulled his phone records."

"Detective, you can't do that without a subpoena!"

"I know! I know! I just wanted to see if I could build anything."

"This better be damn good, detective!"

"On the day Ms. Montago vanished, Boatwright got a call from a payphone at the bus stop right outside the hospital. Then he called an Alexia Campbell in Florida. I think he helped Ms. Montago escape."

Lieutenant Sanders leaned forward in his seat with a stern expression on his face. "Detective Moore, Chicago has a murder rate that seems to be growing at an uncontrollable pace at this very moment and you're using illegal resources to track down someone who hasn't been suspect of anything but being a missing person! Close the gotdamn case, Detective Moore, and go out and arrest some fucking murderers! I don't want to hear anything else about it, period! Goodbye, detective."

Chapter 26

"Uhn-uhn, Ty, where the fuck you think you about to go? You ain't 'bout to go no muthafuckin' where! Been running wild in them streets with Rico crazy ass!"

"Trecey, I ain't trying to hear all that shit, man!" Ty replied.

"Too bad!" Trecey yelled back. "Because what you need to be hearing is that I've been in here raising *your* bad ass children while you out doin' you like you do you!"

"Man, chill out with all that, being extra and shit," Ty sort of warned.

"Whatever nigga," she barked back.

Ty wasn't into the whole family life. He felt he was just too young. At times he made it seem as if Trecey had tricked him all four times she'd gotten pregnant. Some days he had love for her, and other days she was just his *baby mama.*

"I'm 'bout to hit the turf. I'll be back through," he mumbled.

"Tonight, Ty!"

He just shook his head from agitation and opened the door.

"I bet cha ass will wanna stay up in this pussy when you find out another dick jumping up and down in it," she pouted.

Ty stopped mid-stride. "What?" he snapped.

"You heard me," she snapped back.

Before her comment could leave her mouth completely, he had her neck in the palm of his hand. His grip was tenacious. She wrapped both her hands around his wrist for relief.

"Bitch, don't ever disrespect a real nigga! I'll choke you the fuck out, for real!"

Trecey was used to his anger, but could never get used to being choked, especially not when death became a real possibility. Ty released his grip and Trecey crumbled to the floor. He stood over her, watching as she flopped and fidgeted for oxygen.

"You almost killed me, Ty," she whined.

"Almost," he replied with an evil expression. "Just wait and see what happens when I catch that nigga's dick jumping up and down in my pussy!"

Trecey quickly made a mental note to never say anything like that again.

"I'm out," he added, walking out the door.

Ty lived just behind the gas station on Mercy Drive, in the first set of apartments. In each branch of apartments, the Mercy Drive Clique had some sort of drug operation. If the customer needed anything from prescription pills to heroin, the Mercy Drive Clique had it. And if Rico didn't see enough profit coming out of any specific building, then he would send a group of young niggas through to rob anyone who was on their own independent hustle. The crew of young guys called themselves Dem Youngins and Ty was a part of that group.

"Damn, ain't nobody out this bitch tonight," he mumbled to himself as the dope fiends came sporadically.

He positioned himself on the front steps of the apartments and got ready for another night of hustling.

After an hour of slow grinding, Ty saw a walk that he knew could not belong to a junkie. The walk had entirely too much bop in it. Ty patted his waist, assuring himself that his tool was on his belt.

"Aye, Joe, who got that good?" the guy asked.

Ty tried to see if he recognized the face. Something wasn't right.

"Joe?" Ty questioned. "Naw, my nigga, my name ain't Joe. And what you talkin' 'bout, good? Ain't nothing happenin' 'round here. Fuck is you, the police, nigga?" Ty snapped.

The stranger laughed. "Police?" he questioned. "Naw, Cholly! But peep this, fam. There's a person we both have interest in." The man held up his hands in mock surrender as he continued. "Wait! Hold on, Joe! Let me finish. You want him dead, right?"

Ty looked around for an ambush.

"The nigga from GODN?" The stranger asked.

"What's your interest in him?" Ty countered.

Before Ty could figure out what was going on, the stranger had pulled out a gun. Then an all-black Econo van came barreling toward them with the headlights off. The door opened and three other men jumped out with blue bandanas across their faces. They snatched Ty up and threw him inside. He was stripped of all of his possessions, including his clothes. No one said a word.

Twenty minutes later, he was being escorted into an abandoned building.

"Come on, man! Please don't kill me!" Ty pled for the millionth time.

Still he couldn't get one word out of the gunmen. He could tell that they were gang members by the way they all had blue bandanas. Ty was a literal example of the TV series *Naked and Afraid*. He now regretted all of the gangster shit he'd done throughout his life.

The sound of hard bottom shoes sounded throughout the abandoned building. The gunmen spread out to allow the grand entrance of their leader. Ty stayed on his knees, looking around. When the person in the hard-bottoms came into view, Ty almost started crying.

Crusher walked up to him and slapped him to the concrete. "You're the first of your crew, and Rico will be the last that we get," he announced, and then harked a wad of spit onto Ty's face.

Crusher wiped dribbles of spit from his mouth with the back of his hand while staring at Ty. In that moment, the building's garage slid open and another van pulled in. The door opened and another Mercy Drive Clique member was kicked from it with his hands tied.

"Twon," Ty yelled.

Ty noticed that Twon had been beaten. They slid him across the floor and laid him next to Ty. Crusher walked up on him.

"Nigga, you better kill me 'cause Lord knows my dawgs gon' fuck you around," Twon snapped.

Crusher slapped him in between words and spit in his face.

"Mercy Drive is officially dead!" Crusher announced.

Chapter 27

"Life," Pastor Ross bellowed over the microphone. "Life is defined as the period from birth to death, a specific phase of earthly existence. During that existence, we receive precious gifts from our Father in Heaven, which we call blessings! Those of us who thrive to believe in the Word wake up every day understanding that our existence at that very moment was written well before our earthly arrival! Therefore, we consider ourselves blessed. Being able to sleep at night knowing that those blessings were set in motion when Jesus Christ was executed so that the rest of God's children could be... Blessed!" Pastor Ross passionately yelled.

He paused for effect. He wanted his sermon to resonate amongst those in attendance.

"Now, how can any individual go as far as to ignore, disregard, and blatantly disrespect such an honorary gift of life granted by our Father? Who?" Pastor Ross yelled while slamming his palm on the podium.

Cries and soft wails sifted through the church.

"To put one of God's children through what Alexia Campbell endured is tragically vile, morally despicable, physically repulsive, and most of all cowardly! But who am I to judge?"

The church was full. A lot had family ties while others just wanted to see who the video vixen was that had been gunned down. The citizens of the city of Orlando were in full panic due to the extreme increase in violent deaths. Tears fell and empathetic remorse filled the hearts of most, if not all, of those in attendance, aside from one lone soul.

Although the argument as to whether or not she should go to the funeral caused tempers to flair, Siren felt that the least she could do to repay the woman who had taken her in at her lowest point was to see Alexia off. Crusher was against it completely, but Siren was adamant. So there she sat at the back of the church dressed in black attire.

Siren felt as though the pastor's words were meant for her. She'd given up on all aspects of God long before she could verify His existence. Talk of God in the Montago household wasn't all that memorable. She'd turned her nose up at the notion of God the moment her father put his hands on her in a sexual way. She figured it would be better to deny the existence of God than to believe he existed and blame him for all of her misfortunes.

"People, we have no choice but to recognize that we are being invaded by the hosts of Satan," Pastor Ross preached. "Even right here in God's domain! Satan has sauntered into the hearts of some of those *right* here, right next to you! And in his demonic waltz, he has convinced those that *God ain't real* or… or *God don't care about you.* Look at the girl in that casket! If you fall victim to the unbelief, then you too will be a host! But your outcome will be far, far, far worse than just the end of human existence. What Satan refuses to tell you is that God's spirit is released from the shell of human flesh and that death is just protocol. Eternal bliss with God is what follows the release from the human body! Yes! Yes! The fools who destroyed Ms. Campbell's body did a *human* injustice, inhumane to the community but protocol to the creator! Don't fret, God-fearers! Don't mourn excessively, family and friends! Alexia Campbell is in a better situation than any person on earth may assume. It is written. Satan can't win! The deck is stacked against him! If I may suggest anything, it would be that you don't gamble against God!"

The mourners praised his words with applause. Siren just sat there like the odd participant with her eyes hidden behind designer frames. The eulogy was ended and everyone began to evacuate the church, heading for the cemetery. Siren didn't even consider attending the burial. The love of her life was waiting outside for her.

Something caught her eye as she stood to exit the pews. She looked back quickly and her body froze. Staring at her from Alexia's mother's shoulder was the person who had helped her escape Chicago.

Carlos stood erect over his Aunt Janice. Siren didn't know what to say. She'd gotten so used to simply running when she couldn't handle a situation that she followed her usual routine. She respectfully excused herself through the crowd and out of the church.

Carlos couldn't believe it. He thought that she was the girl that had been gunned down with Alexia. "Excuse me, Aunt Janice," he said while removing himself from her grip.

He made his way down the aisle, skipping through the attendees. "Excuse me! Excuse me! Excuse me," he chanted, getting to the front of the church.

Once outside, he stood on the church's steps, scouring the multitudes of people leaving.

He finally spotted her. "Siren," he yelled.

"Damn," she moaned.

"Siren, it's me! It's me, Carlos!"

She stopped. Crusher sat behind heavily tinted windows so she couldn't tell whether or not he was paying attention.

"Oh my God, Siren! I thought you were with her when... when..."

"It was terrible," Siren jumped in.

The pregnant pause between them was strange and uncomfortable.

"I really don't know what happened exactly, but I couldn't believe what I saw," Siren replied.

"Well who was the other girl?" he asked.

Siren removed her designer frames. "I have no clue. I'd never seen her before. Carlos, Alexia was into a lot of things. A lot," she reiterated.

"So... I don't know what to say. I mean, like, are you situated? Do you have somewhere to stay?" he inquired.

"Not situated, but I'll make it. I'm definitely sorry this happened. But thank you for lending me this opportunity. Without you, I don't know where I would be," she explained.

"Siren!" Crusher called out.

Carlos and Siren both looked toward the car. The window was halfway down. Carlos leaned down to see who the deep baritone voice belonged to.

"It was nice seeing you, Carlos. I have to go," Siren announced while putting her glasses back on.

"But I..." he began to say before she cut him off.

"Sorry, I gotta go now," she closed.

"Siren? Siren" his voice trailed her.

He stood there knowing that he'd assisted a woman who had killed. Although it was for a reason, the fact remained that she was a murderer. As he watched her get into the car, he could only wonder why she'd *really* fled Chicago in such a rush. Was she being pursued for something much more heinous than she'd told him? He was actually entertaining the thought of contacting the authorities to report Siren Montago.

"Who was that?" Crusher asked.

Siren had already given him a storyline that did not include Carlos nor did it include the fact that she was from Chicago.

"Oh, that was Alexia's cousin, Carlos," she truthfully stated. "I was just telling him that God was in the mix and that he shouldn't worry about this life because the afterlife is the best thing to come for Alexia," she lied, using an excerpt from Pastor Ross' sermon.

Crusher smiled and sulked in the realization that Siren could be the best addition to his life and the best representation of him. But what he didn't know, what neither of them knew, was that her past was about to unfold in drastic measure.

"I owe you my life, babe," Siren said once the car lurched forward.

Crusher looked over at her and then back at the road. "Why you say that?" he asked.

"Because, had you not stepped in at that video shoot, I would have been the third dead girl in that house."

He looked over at her again. This time he grabbed her hand. "I'm glad I did," he added.

The two headed back toward the hideaway they'd been ducked off in. Crusher's instincts were slacking drastically because of his feelings for Siren and he failed to realize that they were being followed.

Because of Siren Montago, Detective Alfred Moore had taken a vacation from Chicago's precinct to follow Carlos Boatwright to Florida. And behold, he was now following the woman Carlos had lied and said he knew nothing about.

Chapter 28

Detective Moore had a very strong gut feeling about Carlos Boatwright and his involvement with Siren Montago. Although he had been warned by the lieutenant of the homicide department to leave the situation alone, his gut feeling was too strong to ignore.

One thing that he had kept to himself was that while he and his lieutenant were at Carlos' home, he recalled Carlos' wife telling him that he had an urgent phone call from Florida. That, along with the call on Carlos' phone records to Florida on the day of Siren's disappearance, gave Detective Moore a hunch. So he called the number on the phone record, Alexia Campbell, and found out that she'd recently been murdered.

From that initial hunch, he decided to take some vacation time to follow Carlos around for a few days. And it paid dividends. He knew he couldn't use any of the information he'd obtained, but he could surely lure Siren Montago back to Chicago with a little bluffing.

He followed the heavily tinted car for about forty-five minutes. Finally, the car pulled into a gated condominium community. He parked in a parking lot across the street at a Publix Plaza and ran into the community.

"Damn! This fucking place is huge," he panted.

It took him an hour to find the car. His intent wasn't to find out which condo she had entered, but where the car was so he could put a GPS tracking device on it. He had a vacation to enjoy. Luckily for him, the Howard Johnson Hotel was only three quarters of a mile from the community. He was just getting settled around 11:00 pm when the GPS monitor began blinking.

"Shit!" Detective Moore barked.

He fought recklessly to get from under the comforter. He didn't want to let her get too far. He grabbed his shoes and his wind breaker. Patrons watched him run down the hall with only sneakers, boxer shorts, and a Chicago Police windbreaker.

"What is *he* doing?" one older white lady asked her husband.

"Freaky as people are these days, I'm willing to bet we don't really want to know," her husband's shaky voice replied.

Detective Moore followed the GPS tracker for an hour before he realized the location the tracker had given him was incorrect. It had led him to an abandoned building.

"What the…?" he mumbled while shaking the tracker. "Damn! Come onnn," he pouted.

No sooner than he fired up the engine, the door of the building opened and a black van zoomed out. He killed his engine and ducked down in his seat. They didn't see him.

"What in the hell is going on in this motherfucker?" he asked aloud.

He took another look at the GPS and it blinked in the same place. It wasn't broken, the car Siren Montago had been in earlier that day was inside. He thought about what he was wearing and his clothing, or lack thereof, discouraged him from moving for a moment.

"Fuck it," he coached himself.

Wearing only a police jacket, tennis shoes, and boxers, he exited the car. His gun would be the only thing that would give him confidence. The Floridian night air was humid and mosquito filled. It was the kind of weather that screamed *night pool party*! Contrary to the Chicago weather he was used to, the heat and humidity had the jacket already producing sweat. But that didn't discourage Detective Moore as he ran over to the building. The only window to the building had been spray-painted. However, there was one little spot about the size of an eyelash that appeared to have been scraped. He anxiously looked through the small slither of clear glass.

"What the fuck?" he whispered to himself.

Chapter 29

"Aye, bitch, stop callin' my gotdamn phone! I told your ass I don't know where dat nigga at! Shit! Stop callin' my fuckin' phone! I'm tellin' you," Rico barked into the phone.

Frustration was getting the best of him. His crew was hiding from him. He thought they all felt like he had gotten way off course with all the drama. Police were cluttering the city like crazy. Most of the projects were whispering his name so he knew snitching would become a problem real soon.

"Scary ass niggas," he growled, leaning back in his recliner.

Rico thought he heard something. His eyebrows bunched together and he quickly leaned forward. He fumbled with the remote control to turn the TV down. Then he froze. It was his car alarm going off.

"Fuck going on?" he snapped.

He snatched the blinds to the side and looked out.

"Bitch ass nigga," he yelled through the window.

Someone was sitting on the roof of his car and, from the looks of it, had shattered the windshield.

"Nigga got me super fucked up 'round this bitch," Rico barked, grabbing his assault rifle.

He snatched the door open and charged out into the morning air, only to be knocked out by the brute force of a crowbar across his forehead. Rico stiffened with his arms out in front of him and hit the concrete just as fast as the crowbar hit him.

"Damn, Joe! You ain't kill 'em, did you?" one of the Chicago gang members jokingly asked from behind his bandana.

Derrick snatched the assault rifle off of the ground and tossed it back into the home.

"Naw, this nigga good," Derrick replied as he and another member picked Rico up and carried him to the awaiting van.

When they arrived back at the abandoned building, they saw that Crusher was there. That was the first time Derrick had been that close to one of the top men in his organization. Once the van was securely inside the building, Derrick jumped out and signaled for help. Rico was still unconscious. They pulled him out of the van and dropped him in front of his captured comrades.

All hope was gone for the Mercy Drive Clique as they witnessed the head of their organization lay before them unconscious.

Hard bottom shoes crashed against the concrete and stopped in front of the sleeping leader of the group.

"Wake up, baby boy," Crusher sang while crouch down beside Rico.

He palmed Rico's chin and shook it violently. "Time to get up, big man. Wake up!" he added with a couple of swift slaps.

Rico's eyelids fluttered and then popped wide open in shock. "Wha... huh... wha... Wait! Wait," he pled blindly.

He was greeted with a hefty smile from Crusher. "How's everything? You were the last to arrive at the party. Your home boys been waiting. Help this nigga sit up," Crusher demanded.

When Rico was finally able to focus, he saw that his whole crew was naked and tied up. He looked back at Crusher.

"That's all of them! All of them!" Crusher said, standing with his hands in his pockets. "Rico, I gave you the best advice I've ever given anyone who felt the need to harm anything with my stamp on it. You killed not one, but four of *my* employees! And I warned you, nigga. I told you! You remember?"

"Nigga, fuck you," Rico barked.

Crusher smiled. "This is what I said: *Power isn't gained by the opponent you beat. It's gained when you warn the opponent of his demise before you beat 'em.* Either you wasn't listening or you didn't give a fuck! Now, Rico, I'm a man of different avenues, hated by a few and loved by a nation. My word isn't all I have, but it is a prized possession that's priceless to me, especially in the world we live in. So I won't tarnish it for nothing in the world!"

"Kill me, nigga! I ain't scared of no nigga," Rico snapped.

Crusher reached back and slapped Rico, landing his hand flush on Rico's jaw. He followed that up by spitting in his face.

"Stupid ass nigga, that's why all of you niggas are in this situation right now. You don't listen! You been dead since you pointed that gun at me!" Crusher said in a gritted whisper.

The sound of guns loading echoed. Then they were aimed at the Mercy Drive Clique. Blue bandanas and all sorts of guns filled the area all around them.

"I have one person who needs to tell you something. I'm sparing you for at least twenty-four hours. Any time within that twenty-four your number may be called. Be ready!" Crusher laughed.

He began to walk away and then stopped abruptly. "Aye, Rico, I keep enough bullets!"

Chapter 30

Life was pretty routine for the Montago family and Siren had adjusted to the realization of what was for her. As normal, her mother prepared for work. Siren lay under her covers staring at the ceiling with a mind full of teenage thoughts. Not normal fifteen-year-old thoughts, but thoughts that had been developed by her circumstances.

"Eva?" Siren whispered softly. "Eva?"

Siren waited for an answer. When she didn't get a response, she felt sure that her sister was sound asleep. She sneakily shimmied from the bed. The headlights from her mother's car beamed on the ceiling of her bedroom. A quick peek outside assured her that her mom was gone for the next twelve hours.

"Eva?" she whispered again.

There was still no answer. Siren was now confident that Eva was asleep. She took her panties off from under the long t-shirt she wore and tip-toed out of her bedroom. Her parents' bedroom door was cracked. She tip-toed over to the door and peeked in. Her father was also sleeping. Siren quickly looked over her shoulder and then entered. Her father reeked of alcohol, which she could smell as soon as she entered the room.

She took her t-shirt off standing next to the bed. Her hormones had begun to match her abuse. She reached her hand under the comforter and found her intended target. She pulled her father's manhood through the slit in his boxer shorts and began massaging it until it started to stiffen. Feeling his member transform from soft to hard in her hand seemed to arouse her more than it did him.

"Mmm hmm," he moaned while still asleep.

She knew he probably thought he was in a deep dream. She kissed his lips softly. By this time, his manhood was as hard as concrete. He gyrated automatically to the sensation. This added to her own arousal. She slipped under the cover and straddled his stomach. She leaned forward, kissing his neck. She wanted to be loved. She scooted down toward his waist. His manhood poked her just under the mouth of her vagina. He steel had yet to awaken. She reached underneath herself to position his shaft. She tried backing down on it for it to enter her, but her undeveloped body wouldn't allow it. When she forcefully tried getting it inside, he woke up.

"What the... Siren!" he yelped.

She covered his mouth with her hand and looked toward the door.

"Shhh! Daddy, be quiet!" she said.

"What are you doing?" he whispered after forcing her hand from his mouth.

She rocked her hips side to side, trying to get his manhood inside of her. The tip finally slid in and they both gasped from the sensation. His eyes bulged and the realization of what was happening registered.

"No!" he snapped, tossing her small body off of him.

She tried to get back in position but he jolted from the bed in haste. She followed in a hormone induced scramble.

"Please," she begged, grabbing his waist.

He slapped her to the ground. His intensity diminished as he stood there huffing in disbelief and she lay on the floor holding the side of her face. The two didn't say one word. She slowly climbed to her feet. She was no longer feeling comfortable naked. Her body withered as she eagerly put her nightshirt back on.

"Siren," *he whispered apologetically.*

It was no use. Without another thought or word, she bolted out of the room.

Siren's eyes fluttered open from the dream. There was no emotion, just the same thought that she had after every dream, which was the most obvious one. How could a parent sexually assault their own child?

She took a deep breath and a surge of queasiness churned in her chest. Placing her hand between her breasts, she realized that trying to calm the feeling was useless. She sat upright and instantly began wrestling with the sheets that seemed to be trying to stop her movement. Finally, her feet touched the floor, yet she couldn't move them as fast as she needed to. She clamped her hands over her mouth, but the vomit wasn't trying to be slowed. Vomit spewed recklessly from the crevices around her hands as she raced to the bathroom. She made it just in time to do nothing but dry heave. Her naked body hugged the toilet tightly.

"Ugh! Ugh!" she panted as the dry heaves subsided.

The sound of the alarm system beeped, letting her know that Crusher had just gotten back in.

"Siren," he called out.

"I'm in the bathroom," she responded.

He walked in and saw her naked on the floor. His eyes followed the trail of vomit out of the bathroom. He lifted his foot, seeing that he was standing in the middle of it.

"Damn! You sick?" he asked.

"Yeah," she groaned. "I don't know what it is."

A quick rundown of possibilities crossed his mind and the most obvious one resounded. He ignored it completely, or as much as he could.

"I have something to show you, but from the looks of it..." He burst into laughter before he could finish his statement.

"Get out of here," she pouted.

He laughed and left so she could get herself together.

"What is it that you have to show me?" she asked, coming out of the bathroom.

Crusher pulled a .45 automatic from the back of his waistband.

"Here," he said.

She looked down at the gun in his hand. It was the same gun that she had used to kill Rico's partner, Angelo. Her piercing eyes looked up from the gun.

"There's someone who's been dying to see you," Crusher responded with a grin.

Chapter 31

"Shit! Alfred, mannn, what have you gotten into?" Detective Moore whispered to himself while staring through the slither in the abandoned building's window.

A revving engine sounded from a distance. He looked back and he could see headlights coming down the street. He ran into a ticket of bushes. No sooner then he could get totally hidden, a van turned into the property. The headlights flashed at the building and someone from inside opened the garage doors.

"Fuck," he mumbled.

He patted his jacket pocket for his phone to capture a picture. But he'd left it in his room. His mind roamed curiously as to why there were armed men wearing blue bandanas standing around the building. And why was all this activity taking place in the early morning hours?

Moments passed and there was no more movement outside. He couldn't hear anything going on inside. His police instincts kicked in. He just had to see what was going on in that building. He took off from the thicket to the back of the building as the gravel crumbled loosely under his sneakers. The windows were too high for him to see in. He continued to scramble around the building looking for access. He caught a break when he noticed some used tires at the back of the building. Excitement turned to energy as he stacked them and climbed on top.

"Come onnn," he whined in frustration.

He was just a few inches short. Darkness smothered every inch around him. With no flashlight, he was out of luck.

The light from inside the building illuminated the structure of the window. With that, he could see a small ledge on the window structure that he could use to pull himself up. He tucked his gun in his jacket pocket, tested the strength of the structure, and pulled. If he could have seen how old the building looked to be, he wouldn't have attempted such an inconceivable act. The structure collapsed.

"Umph," he grunted as his back hit the gravel.

Adrenaline moved to his body on autopilot. He didn't know if he had been hurt or not but there was one thing he did know, he couldn't be caught states away investigating something his boss had told him to disengage. He ran faster with that thought in mind. He closed in on his vehicle and the garage doors growled as they open behind him. There was no way his legs would move any faster. Shock had him believing that a bunch of wild tigers were licking at his heels. The rental car was right there. Then the unthinkable happened, he fell down.

"Nooo! No! No! Get up," he coached himself.

Fortunately, he was able to regain footing and dive into his car. He peeked up just in time to see the car Siren Montago had gotten into earlier pass by. He quickly turned the ignition, put the car in drive, and panicked. He patted his pockets for his gun. It was gone.

Chapter 32

Carlos' heart shattered even more as he sat in his cousin Alexia's childhood room at his Aunt Janice's house. All of her pictures were full to capacity with joy, smiles, laughter, and life. He couldn't fathom life without her around. She was always the upbeat one, bursting at the seams with ambition. She never limited success to just one wish. She was adventurous, willing to *get it at all costs*.

A smile crossed his lips briefly, and then abruptly dissipated. Why would someone, anyone, do that to her?

Siren Montago was the name that was pulsating through his brain like a *Breaking News* flash. Her bright, eerie green eyes were vivid in his mind. He could see them as clearly as if she were standing before him. He had helped her at the drop of a dime, without even knowing her, and he could only cringe at the bland explanation she'd given him with regards to what had happened to his cousin.

"Carlos, Alexia was involved in a lot of things, a lot!" he recalled her saying.

The fact that there was no courtesy or emotion in her explanation hurt more than anything. It seemed to him that the only person who could provide any input on his cousin's death was much less interested in elaborating a theory than riding off into the sunset with her new little boyfriend.

Jealousy sort of nipped at the edges of his emotions. In truth, he'd had an instant crush on Siren the moment her soft words poured from her lips. Her captivating eyes and perfect frame only added to her appeal.

"Fuck this," he mumbled, aggressively reaching for his wallet.

He dug out the card and stared at it as if he was in a western standoff. A photo essay of all the encounters he'd had with Siren, from the moment his truck crashed into her all the way to the point he stood watching her leave him standing in front of the church with a world of questions, flooded his mind. A deep exhale poured through his nose. He curled his lips inside his mouth. Just above the business card he was staring at he could see Alexia's big pretty smile, enjoying life at the *Wet-N-Wild* water park. Memories of her would not quell, no matter how hard his mind tried to entertain other thoughts. After another deep exhale, he plopped down on the bed, dug his cell phone from his pocket, and finally dialed the number on the card.

"Detective Moore, how can I help you?"

Carlos looked at Alexia's cheerleading picture on the wall, which caused his eyes to glaze over with emotion.

"I'm calling about Siren Montago," Carlos' voice cracked in defeat.

"Who am I speaking with?" the detective asked.

"Carlos Boatwright."

"Mr. Boatwright," Detective Moore yelped with wonder. "You mentioned the Montago case."

"Yes, it would be nice if I could come see you to talk to you about this face to face. But I can't because I'm down in Florida for my little cousin's funeral," Carlos explained.

Detective Moore continued to act unaware. "Is it that important?" Moore asked.

Carlos closed his eyes. "I'm afraid so."

"Well hit me with what you got. Maybe I can assist you in some way," Detective Moore countered.

"Actually, it's simple, detective. Siren Montago is down here in Florida. I even spoke with her. Now the hard part is explaining how, in fact, she got here."

"Do you know where she's at?" Detective Moore asked.

"Not really, but I know the license plate number of the car she got into. Plus, I need to tell you the reason she *really* had to leave Chicago," Carlos confided.

"Is it safe for me to assume that she vanished with your help?"

"Yes," Carlos replied full of guilt.

"Good! Now I have a valid reason to arrest you if need be," Detective Moore blackmailed.

"Arrest?" Carlos yelped. "What for?"

"You have a GPS on your phone?" Moore asked.

"Yes, but…" Carlos began but was rudely cut off by the detective.

"About forty-five minutes from where you're at, there's a hotel. Write this down, Howard Johnson Hotel just off of Interstate 4. Exit in a town called Lakeland."

He paused to let Carlos jot down the info.

"The street it's on is Lakeland Boulevard," Moore added.

"Got it," Carlos replied. "But what do I…"

"Go there now and call me when you get there," Moore said, cutting him off again. "I followed you, Mr. Boatwright. I know more than you think I know. I am a detective. Hurry up! I'm waiting."

Carlos heard the call drop and he damn near gagged from the dry sandpaper feeling in his throat.

Chapter 33

Crusher sat in the designated parking spot that the condominium association provided with purchase. Everything had wound back down. GODN Entertainment was shining in Atlanta as if nothing had happened. He was very satisfied with how his team found ambition in everything they did. So much was being created under their imprint. The hard work and good judgment had paid off. But there was one thing outside of wiping Rico and his clique off the face of the earth that he had to deal with.

Of all the obstacles life had thrown toward him and he'd hurdled, he'd never been able to face this one thing. This was what he'd run from his entire life. Looking at all of his close friends who were entangled in relationships, and watching them lead a three-way life of business, marriage, and lifestyle, always turned him away from the mere thought of it. He'd done an excellent job of avoiding it altogether. That was until a one Siren Montago came into his life.

He shook his head at how she'd unintentionally fell into his lap. She was a real bitch, he felt. A feminine beauty with the soul of a madman, she was ideal for any gangster in the whole world. But he sat in his car thinking deeply about his choices. He hated additions.

"Stick with what got you to where you're at," he told himself on many occasions. Yet he sat in his car pondering his choices, choices that should never have been part of a gangster's mentality.

He grabbed the small CVS bag and made his way into the condominium. He could hear the Isley Brothers' *Choosy Lover* pouring from the speakers as soon as the door opened.

Siren hadn't slept well all night so he knew she was probably comatose. But to his surprise, she was up. She was lying across the bed, but she was awake.

"Hey!" he greeted while lying gently onto her back. "Feel better?"

"Kind of," she whispered.

He kissed the back of her neck and got up.

"Hey, tonight I want to take you somewhere. I want you to get as jazzed up as you can," he schemed.

"Where we going?" she asked.

"We'll be leaving at about 1:30 in the morning," he replied, completely ignoring her last question.

"Okay," she whispered in her sexy voice.

A few seconds elapsed before she spoke again. "Crusher," she called out, sitting up on the bed. "Can I ask you something?"

"What's up?" he nonchalantly answered.

"This... Us... I mean, what is this we have between us?" she asked.

He looked away in quick thought. "What is it you're getting from me? What's your conscience saying?" he countered.

"Crusher, I've never been in love so I can't tell you that that's the emotion I have. But honestly, I feel whole when you're around me. You know, I came here with absolutely nothing!"

Something in her heart was telling her to explain everything about her past, but the lie had already taken root.

"I never wanted to give myself to anyone before I met you. It scared me how badly I wanted to have you as my first. And now that that's passed, I'm questioning if I made a mistake, like maybe I didn't analyze the situation deeply enough."

"Is that how you feel?" he asked.

"Please don't take offense... I... It's confusing me because I don't know how to say what my mind is telling me. And maybe I'm just a stupid woman, but, Crusher, I want to learn how to make you feel the same way I feel. If this is what love is, then I'm saying I'm in love with you."

He sprang to a standing position, exhaling deeply.

"Love?" he questioned. "What if I told you I don't know how to love? What if I told you that love doesn't resonate in my heart as something soulful, full of solace and sunshine?"

He walked to the bedroom window and looked out. The bright daylight stared back at him. For the first time, the man with all the solutions and answers was drawing a blank.

"Do you want to try?" Siren asked.

"But we barely even know each other," was his only defense.

"I'm lost! Is there a specific time frame on how long it takes for a person to feel a certain way about another person? If so, I need you to tell me how long I have to wait. What I'm feeling isn't going anywhere. That is unless you feel totally different about this," she added.

He looked at the bag on the dresser from CVS.

"I tell you what, we can go further under one condition," he replied.

"What?" she said with a grin, thinking it was sex related.

He grabbed the bag and took the box out.

"See what this says first."

Siren didn't hesitate. She went into the bathroom. Ten minutes later, the door opened.

"Crusher, I'm positive!"

His eyes locked onto the test in her hand.

"You sure?" he questioned.

"Look," she yelped.

The deck was stacked in her favor now.

"Now we can try! I've never loved before, but you having my child will definitely put the words I, love, and you in the same sentence," he replied.

Siren lunged into his arms and buried her face into his chest. He looked over her and out the window. If the bright Florian sun could talk, Crusher would have known that shit was about to get scorching hot.

Chapter 34

"So you're saying that Siren told you that some guys had killed her sister and that the reason you ran into her is because she was being chased by the same guys that had killed her sister?"

"Correct," Carlos agreed.

"Did you see anyone chasing her?" Moore asked.

"Not that I recall. I honestly forgot anything that was going on in that moment," Carlos replied.

Detective Moore knew that it was something crazy about the whole Montago murder. Now he was getting somewhere. And from the looks of it, Siren Montago was becoming number one on the list of suspects.

"Alright, Carlos," Detective Moore began. "There's a dilemma here for the both of us. But there is a way that we can sweep all of this under the rug."

"I'm listening," Carlos countered.

"After I saw you talking to Siren Montago at your cousin's funeral, I followed her. Long story short, I was led to a building with some strange activity going on. In the midst of snooping around the building, I dropped my firearm," Detective Moore explained.

Carlos had no indication of where the conversation was heading.

"I put a tracking device on the car she got into after the funeral and I'm waiting for the car to return so I can find my gun and get back to Chicago.

"Strange activity? Building? Lost your gun? Detective, I don't understand."

"I need some help finding my gun, your help," Moore assured.

"*My* help?" Carlos countered. "My help? With all due respect, you're the cop!"

Detective Moore cringed at the thought of how deeply he'd fallen into this situation. "Okay, then I'm very capable of relaying your confessions and having you indicted on aiding and abetting a murder. And it will stick! Or you can come help me find my gun and go on living your life without a peep from my department. It's your choice!"

"I mean, you can't call for backup from the police department?" Carlos asked.

"And what, Carlos? Tell them that a fucking cop came from Chicago and started an investigation on their turf? Come on, Carlos, use that brain of yours! Actually, this is not up for discussion. Either you're going to help me or I'm arresting you today," he bluffed.

"Carlos plopped back restlessly against the chair he was sitting in. Trying to turn Siren Montago in to the authorities had backfired and now he was in more trouble than he'd bargained for.

"When?" Carlos hopelessly asked.

Detective Moore needed help because it was just too dangerous for him to go alone. The guns he'd seen in the hands of the men at the building were just too big for comfort. Now he had a decoy.

"As soon as this little triangle starts moving," the detective replied, showing Carlos the GPS tracker.

Chapter 35

"Gotdamn, girl, you're wearing the hell outta that dress!"

"You like? It was Alexia's. She let me have it," Siren explained.

Crusher realized the time had neared. It was time to get this obstacle out of the way and try prepping for a life he knew nothing about, with a woman he knew nothing about. He escorted her to the door.

"Hold up," she said. "I forgot the gun."

He smiled on the inside. He could see her eagerness to prove herself. The sight was movie-like, a beautiful woman with a gun in her hand. The ride to the building wasn't dreadful for Crusher, but Siren's heart turned flips. Nothing she'd ever harmed was done premeditatedly. All of her murders were committed because of her reaction in the moment.

For some reason, she was now feeling an extreme desire to love the man driving the car with every fiber of her being.

"You ever been to Atlanta, Georgia?" he asked.

"Nope! I've never been much of anywhere," she replied.

"Atlanta's the city!" he boasted. "I like Orlando, but I was thinking that Atlanta would be more of an area to start a family."

"There's something I have to explain to you before we go on," she started.

He took his eyes off the road for a brisk moment to analyze the sincerity in her face. She stared back at him. He was hoping she wasn't about to dig up some crazy Maury Povich shit. He returned his eyes to the road.

"I'm wanted by some very bad people."

"Wanted?" he questioned.

"Remember when I told you about me killing my dad?"

He nodded in agreement.

"Well, I was deemed incompetent to stand trial and admitted to the psychiatric ward for five years. While I was in there, my mother died and my sister, Eva, became my guardian. Last year, I was released from the ward."

"Last year?" he again questioned.

"The day my sister came to pick me up, I killed her boyfriend, strangled him to death with shoestrings."

Crusher did a double-take. The first look was at her face. The other was at her purse, where the gun was. He wasn't sure where this conversation was headed.

"Not knowing, nor caring about who he was at the time I killed him, I later found out that he must've been a part of some type of organization or group because a group of them killed my sister in revenge! They thought both of us had died but I managed to get out of the burning house."

"Wait! They killed your sister because *you* killed one of their members?" he clarified.

"Yeah. They thought they had both of us!"

"Okay, go ahead," he prompted.

"I was barely able to escape from the house. They had stomped me unconscious and when I woke up, the house was burning and my sister was hog-tied and burning alive!"

"Damn," Crusher cringed.

"Well, I was able to make it out but not far. I collapsed in someone's back yard. When I woke up, I realized that I happened to be in the back yard of the cousin of the guy I'd strangled and killed. He called the goons who had tried to kill me the night before and turned me over to them. I was able to escape by burning the driver in his eye. I ran and was hit by a truck! That put me in the hospital in a coma for six months."

"This shit would make a good ass movie," he joked.

The seriousness in her expression broke his smile.

"You remember the guy that I was talking to at Alexia's funeral?"

Crusher squinted, trying to remember. "Yeah, I remember."

"Well that's who ran me over,' she revealed.

Crusher stiffened.

"The guy I had escaped from was trying to get to me while I was in the coma, but the hospital security wouldn't let anybody in. When I came out of the coma, I called the guy that hit me and he helped me escape. That's how Alexia and I met. That's how I ended up in Orlando."

By the time she'd finished speaking, Crusher was livid.

"So you lied to me?" he questioned.

"I didn't know what to say to you, so I told you bits and pieces so you wouldn't think I was crazy! It had nothing to do with trying to deceive you," she assured.

"You say you're wanted. Well in what city did all of this take place?" he asked.

"Chicago," she answered.

He had to steady the wheel after jerking it.

"Chicago? What part?" he gasped in total shock.

"Right around 127th, over by Burr Oak Cemetery," she said.

"Get the hell outta here!" he replied in amazement. "That's my area!"

Now it was her time to look at him in surprise.

"You're from Chicago?" she panicked.

"Born and raised, it's crazy how small the world is, huh?"

They both grew silent, drifting in their own thoughts.

"Is there *anything* else?" he asked.

"Yeah, there is. I wanted to tell you that I'll be the best friend you never had!"

"I hope so!"

The building had neared, it was in clear view. Crusher's thoughts tumbled around in his head. He was beginning to see that there was a lot to learn about the woman seated next to him. At the same time, he had the prettiest killer known to man. That made the way Rico would die much more appealing. He pulled up to the door and parked outside.

"Listen, when this door opens up, pull in and come to where I'm standing," he said with a smirk as he looked at her purse and then at her.

"After this, we're going to Atlanta," he assured in hopes of making her understand that this wasn't the type of life they would lead.

Siren smiled while placing the gun onto her lap.

Chapter 36

Detective Moore pulled up in time to see someone walk inside the garage door of the abandoned building.

"They're inside!" Moore announced to a scared shitless Carlos.

Detective Moore parked in the same place he had parked the previous time and gave Carlos a flashlight. "Follow me," he ordered.

The two got out and Carlos followed Detective Moore, passing the car they had trailed to the building.

***

Inside the building, something was being discussed that only two men could hear.

"I know this may not be the time, but Mitch wanted me to tell you what happened to one of our guys back in Chicago. I was supposed to tell you as soon as I got here, but I only saw you once," Derrick explained.

Crusher looked at him patiently. He was very good at letting a person talk. Funk looked on, knowing that after they slaughtered the Mercy Drive Clique, he had orders to slaughter Derrick.

Crusher's initial focus was on enjoying the show while he watched a whole squad fall at the hands of a female. But he caught something interesting in Derrick's explanation.

"Wait! You say she burnt your eye with a cigar?" Crusher inquired.

"Yeah, fam, right here. See?" Derrick showed Crusher his scar.

"Did she happen to get away from you and get hit by a truck?" Crusher questioned.

"Damn, Joe, how you know?" Derrick questioned in awe.

He vividly remembered hearing the exact same story just minutes before when Siren told it. She had killed one of his men and was pregnant by the leader whose vow to the organization was to kill anything that brought harm to them. He looked at the garage door, knowing that the woman sitting in his car was wanted by his organization.

In the process of Derrick and Crusher each pondering their views on the situation at hand, a gunshot rang out from the outside of the building.

***

"Carlos!" Siren yelped from behind the car's tinted windows.

Another man that she had never seen before ran close behind him.

"What is he doing?" she asked aloud.

Both men had flashlights and were running around in a sneaky fashion. Siren frantically looked towards the garage door and back in the direction Carlos had run. Her indecisiveness caused her movements to linger like molasses. The gun lay on her lap. The man she was in love with was inside. And seeing Carlos quickly led her to believe that she had to stop whatever was going on. She opened the car door with caution.

The nightlife of the wilderness echoed. Owls hooted, crickets sent shrills of mating calls, accompanied by many other unknown sounds that the darkness seemed to amplify. The eerie moment reeked of suspense. Siren stepped out and listened but nothing could be heard other than the sounds of the night. She looked at the door for any sign of Crusher. Nothing. She walked around the car to the side of the building. Darkness consumed everything. Then she noticed a flashlight beam in the distance and, suddenly, a gunshot rang out.

She clung to the side of the building, looking toward the sound. She could hear the scuffling of shoes trying to grip the gravel.

"Go! Go!" a male's voice echoed.

The running got closer. She stood and positioned herself in their path. Light from a far off streetlamp shone on half of her body. The sound of the garage door crashed open and the footsteps of the gangsters inside poured out in her direction. Siren felt comfort knowing her man was in that group. She wrapped her finger around the trigger as Carlos and the man with him skidded to a stop.

"Siren!" Crusher called out.

"Siren," Carlos pouted.

"Siren Montago," Detective Moore said, pointing his gun in the direction of the men who were approaching.

"Funk, this that bitch! That's her!" Derrick yelled, raising his gun toward her.

Funk followed Derrick's lead. Guns were pointed in every direction.

"Hold up!" Crusher yelled a millisecond after a fatal shot was fired. Everyone's mouth fell open in shock as they realized whose life the bullet had taken.

To be continued...

Made in the USA
Coppell, TX
14 April 2023

15618393R00118